"Angela, in her relatively short life, has been faced with more than her share of incredible circumstances, any one of which could have changed her outlook on life. We have watched our niece not only endure but triumph over these challenges with a continuing positive attitude and an abiding trust in God. Indeed, it is her faith that has carried her through. By sharing her experiences in *Miracles in Action*, she provides encouragement and inspiration to all of us to rise above our losses and misfortunes and live our lives to the fullest."

—Marilyn McCoo & Billy Davis Jr., Grammy award-winning
    artists, formerly of The Fifth Dimension

"Angela Alexander shares a personal story of loss and redemption. Anybody who has ever gone through a tough time will be able to relate and take powerful lessons and insights from these pages. This is a must read for anyone looking to make it beyond the pain of loss and heartache."

—Les Brown, award-winning speaker and best-selling author
    of *Live Your Dreams* and *It's Not Over Until You Win*

"This is a must-read book. . . . Angela shares openly and honestly from her own personal experiences about how to travel the road of hardship to the highway of healing, which is the victory that God has so richly blessed her with. This book serves as an inspiration to those dealing with issues ranging from family forgiveness to the passing of loved ones. You see, overcoming a situation is only part of the healing process; true victory is evident only in the lives of those who are able to share their testimony with others."

—Pastor Diego Mesa, Abundant Living Family Church

MIRACLES
IN ACTION

Turning Pain into Power
and Grief into Peace

ANGELA ALEXANDER

RUNNING SPRINGS PRESS

Library of Congress Control Number: 2008931673

ISBN : 978-0-9778472-0-4

Published by Running Springs Press
P.O. Box 463
Etiwanda, California 91739
Website: www.miraclesinaction.com
E-mail: miraclesinaction@yahoo.com

10 9 8 7 6 5 4 3 2 1

This book is dedicated to my sister Alice for her sacrifice. She prepared my life; she saved my life.

To my sons, Murice and Roger, for not only listening but also for obeying God's word. Now many will be helped through their words.

To my husband, Surie, and my daughters, Angela and Angelina. Thank you for being patient with me. Thank you for understanding how important writing this book was to me and for me.

CONTENTS

Foreword   xi

Preface   xiii

Author's Note   xvii

Special Thanks   xix

Chapter 1   Unexpected News   1

Chapter 2   Seeds of Destiny   5

Chapter 3   My "Lonely" Soldier   23

Chapter 4   In Sickness and in Health   35

Chapter 5   Life Worth Celebrating   55

Chapter 6   Déjà Vu   63

Chapter 7   Alice in Wonderland   69

Chapter 8   Forgiveness   87

Chapter 9   Moving Forward   97

Chapter 10   Miracles in Action   113

Chapter 11   My Peace Is Complete   133

Chapter 12   A Peace Bigger than Me   153

Chapter 13   Deciding to Fly   165

Chapter 14   Trials, Tribulations, and Triumph   183

Chapter 15   Achieving Our Dreams   193

Photographs follow pages 152 and 211

FOREWORD

It wasn't merely by chance that all of my daughters were born on the same day of the week—except Angela. Neither the doctor, called away from his Sunday church service, nor I knew what a wonderful spirit we were assisting into this physical realm.

During my daughter's childhood, I never really noticed that distinctive difference in her; after all, I thought all eight of my children were unique. In the last decade or two, I have noticed more of Angela's light shining, especially through times and events that could have destroyed not only her and her family, but also, more importantly, her spirit.

This book takes us beyond just the talking, the listening, the wishing, and praying phases. Here, we experience a sermon that is lived on the cutting edge of a new paradigm in our society: how we experience "loss" and how we express "love." Angela says yes to Life, and the response is clearly seen in her smile. She has refused to be a victim of the human conditions and of her circumstances.

Have you ever wondered how to handle a heartbreaking event in your life? Have you ever experienced trying times, or are you even now in the midst of barely holding on day to day? This book will allow you to reflect upon those experiences and to find simple supportive strength for your own help, hope, humor, and inner healing.

—Julia Jean, Angela's Mother

PREFACE

Miracles in Action is echinacea for the soul. Like the immune system booster echinacea, this book is spiritual medicine. Angela Alexander has presented for dissection insight into the attitudes we need to uphold when life's challenges threaten to overtake us.

Although I met Mrs. Alexander during the school year of 1998, it seems our souls met long before. At that time, I was a fifth grade teacher. I remember meeting Mr. and Mrs. Alexander as loving parents of their two children, Angela and Murice. The Alexander's children were model students—they had a zest for life, a love of others, and with their daily smiles, they were easy to fall in love with.

As the time passed, my role changed. My office changed from a classroom to the front office, where I served as assistant principal. The Alexander family also changed. The love God blessed them to have and their talent and patience in raising children afforded them the opportunity to become foster parents of another beautiful daughter and another handsome son. During these days, our relationship grew. Mrs. Alexander could often be seen accompanying her husband, Surie, as they continually volunteered as parent helpers around the school. Since that time, I have come to love the entire family.

I will never forget the day the busses were stuck in traffic, trying to return our fourth graders from a field trip. One of those fourth graders was the foster daughter of the Alexanders, Angelina. It was March 31, 2000, a day that allowed us all to enjoy the siblings and parents of our fourth graders as we waited. Precious time was spent enjoying Angela and Surie's children, Murice and Roger. I didn't know at the time how that one day's apparent mishap was actually God's miracle in action.

This book is full of miracles from the beginning to the end. You know, those moments we too often miss because we fail to look beyond the obvious to the Omnipotent. In her wisdom, Angela has cleverly coined her life's definitive phrase, miracles in action, and conveyed her life-changing experiences in a way that guides the reader to transform, transcend, and triumph over apparent adversities. Any reader with the desire, thirst, and basic need for oxygen will find the ability to inhale again as each line is read.

Only after the completion of this masterpiece was the author's life purpose in place. I can say with pride, I am truly appreciative of her willingness to allow God to take over. Alone and in her own time, she found the keys in her soul and allowed me to walk with her as we traveled together through the locked closets in her mind, collecting the gems in those hidden corners that make this masterpiece priceless.

Get ready to breathe. We laughed and we cried. You too will do the same. So get your box of tissue and be prepared to find your keys to unlock the miracles in your life.

—Cecille Walks Peace

AUTHOR'S NOTE

This book is a true and actual account of my life. As you will see as my story unfolds, there were times when I didn't make the best choices. Throughout the years and events in my life, I have come to trust God for everything. It is my hope that the lessons I learned through all my trials and challenges will inspire you and show you that you can turn your pain into power and your grief into peace.

I pray that as you read my story, you will be able to look beyond the times in life when you or I have stumbled and see God's ineffable love and tender mercy at work. His love and forgiveness are truly a miracle in action.

I have quoted Les Brown at the beginning of each chapter in this book. I hope you find his motivational messages as inspiring as I do.

Enjoy!

Be blessed,
Angela Alexander

SPECIAL THANKS

Thank you so very much for your love and contribution toward the many rewrites of my autobiography, *Miracles in Action:* Cecille Walks Peace, Joyce Felix, Julia J. Harris, Sheila Marchbanks, Diamond Andrews, Darlene Ferrona, Candice Burnett with C n' R Images, Sarah Thomas, Aundrea Bradford, Skyla Thomas, Robin Wisser, Stephanie Graham, Vicki Beck, Patricia Traylor, Helen Dotson, Janet Chaikin, editor, and Nigel J. Yorwerth and Patricia Spadaro of PublishingCoaches.com.

CHAPTER ONE

UNEXPECTED NEWS

"When life knocks you down, try to land on your back.
Because if you can look up, you can get up."

April 1, 2000, was no April Fool's Day for me. That day marked the beginning of a new reality, and jokes were the farthest thing from my mind.

After arriving in Japan on military assignment, I called home to let my family know I had landed safely. My son Roger answered the telephone. He was amazed that it was Friday evening where he was, yet on the other side of the world it was already Saturday afternoon. He told me about his Friday fun day at school and how much he enjoyed all the activities. We then exchanged "I love you's." Next I recognized Murice's voice on the telephone. He told me how proud he was of himself for the A he received on his written and oral book report that day. His classmates thought the paper-bag puppet he made was just too cool. We also exchanged "I love you's." I spoke with my girls, Angela and Angelina, and told Surie, my husband, an April

Fool's joke. We exchanged love lines, and then I went for some much-needed sleep.

While I slept, my family began their weekend routine. Saturday afternoon Surie loaded our four children into our five-passenger truck and proceeded to drop off bill payments and run errands from the "Honey-Do" list I had left before heading to Japan for my two-week annual tour with my Air Force Reserve unit.

Our children endured each stop and eagerly awaited their favorite location, the 99 Cent Store, to trade their allowance for candy and toys. That day, Angela, eleven; Angelina, ten; and Roger, eight, bought their usual bag of goodies. Murice, also eight, purchased candy and a small basketball hoop to hang on the back of his bedroom door. Each of them shopped as much for themselves as for the neighborhood friends with whom they shared their goodies. Surely Angela's and Murice's generous giving can only be attributed to Surie's side of the family because, I'll admit, in their shoes, my first inclination would have been to sell the candy and stash the cash. Until then, though, it seemed my tendency for deal making hadn't rubbed off on them.

Nearly their entire day was typical and ordinary until the burgundy car interrupted everything.

Three hours into my twelve-hour shift at Yokota Air Force Base, Captain Mivehchi summoned me from the group. "It wasn't me! I didn't do it! Whatever 'it' was," I thought, heading toward him. He started with small talk about the day's regimen, then led me to an office and closed the door. Inside sat a gentleman in civilian clothes and Technical Sergeant Thomas, a woman from our unit. For a moment, ominous silence filled the small room as each gave me a solemn stare that sent my mind racing to make sense of the unexpected gathering. Finally, Captain Mivehchi broke the stillness. He introduced the man as a priest and motioned for me to be seated. The priest began to read from the Red Cross paperwork that shook nervously in his hands. "Your family has been in a car accident." Slowly and cautiously, he continued. "Your husband . . . he's . . ."

At that moment, I felt as though time had stopped and no one else was in the room. A prayer my children often said before going to bed ran through my mind:

> *Now I lay me down to sleep,*
> *I pray the Lord my soul to keep.*
> *If I should die before I wake,*
> *I pray the Lord my soul to take.*

Not another soul. Not another soul! Weren't there enough souls from my family on the other side already? My two oldest brothers were there. Vincent, at just twenty-seven years old, had been killed instantly in a car crash in Seattle. Barron, at thirty-eight, was shot and killed by the police during a car chase in Arkansas. Not another soul, I thought again. Let this be the April's Fool's joke of the day.

CHAPTER TWO

SEEDS OF DESTINY

"You don't have to be great to get started,
but you do have to get started to be great."

The seventh child is a wonder child," my sister Alice and I overheard someone say when we were children in the 1960s. At once, we eagerly counted aloud on our fingers the order of our siblings' births.

"Sharon…Vincent…Barron…Kevin…Alice…David…Angela…Susan."

Only then did we both realize that God had appointed me as the seventh child.

"I'm the seventh child!" I screamed with excitement.

My sister immediately disputed the result and was sure we messed up somewhere along the way.

"Let's count it again!" she demanded.

After the third recount, my sister boasted instead that she was "Alice in Wonderland."

In my family, I am the "seventh wonder." As I processed the blessing bestowed upon me by my birth order, I stood a little taller, and I claimed the phrase "The seventh child is the wonder child" as my personal slogan. It was a sign to me that great wonders and adventures were destined to be in my life, and I made my decision then and there that it would be so. Of course, each of my siblings is wonderful in his or her own right. However, my life especially, it seems, has been filled with more than its share of incredible circumstances. This simple slogan planted a thought in my head the size of a mustard seed that grew into a strong, meaningful faith.

My family was among the first to infuse our mostly white neighborhood with our version of African-American culture. Neatly manicured lawns were the standard, and quietness blanketed our block of about twenty-one brick homes during the day while parents worked and children learned at school. But during late afternoons, my siblings and I decorated the landscape with a host of "colorful" activities. We introduced our neighbors to bolo bats, jacks, card games, double-Dutch jump rope and filled the air with the soulful sounds of the Jackson Five emanating from our record players and eight-track tape players. The original *Soul Train* made regular stops on our small black-and-white television set as the smell and smoke from oil-pressed hair invaded our playtime and homefront. We lived in a city where winter froze everything except time, and summer blistered every memory of the past winter's frost.

Though there was always lots of food in our St. Louis home, there were equally as many people. So, early on, I learned how to eat with a mission: make haste to the kitchen as the home-cooked meals were prepared. Laggards simply missed out. The food bill never bothered the breadwinner, although I do remember a lock on the freezer door. "I'd rather have a grocery bill than a doctor's bill," my twenty-one-year-old father, Arthur, a strong, muscular, hard-working, good looking and serious man, would often say.

This phrase reminded my mother, Julia—slim ebony princess of medium height—that the money was well spent. She and my father married in 1950 when my mother was a budding sixteen-year-old with long lashes, her eyes milk chocolate brown, sweet and smooth.

It must have been challenging to raise eight children, especially with the first five born only a year apart. But my father had been accustomed to work and large families. The oldest child of seven, he helped care for his six younger siblings. My grandfather drove trucks for a living. Help from his son Arthur allowed for more runs and more profit. Later, my father joined the U.S. Army and drove military vehicles, making good use of the training he had received while growing up.

By the time my mother married my father, he was out of the military but still armed with a healthy work ethic. As an electrician, he changed streetlights for the St. Louis

Lighting Company. An entrepreneur, he turned his passion for cooking into a meals-on-wheels barbecue joint. Instead of beckoning buyers to purchase ice cream, he sold barbecue rib tips, smoked chicken, potato salad, and, as he would say, "sody pop." Then he started Billy's Walk-Up restaurant, where his famous pig's feet and tripe sandwiches were a hit.

When my father moonlighted as a janitor, my siblings and I also worked that shift. We emptied trash baskets, wiped down desks, and vacuumed floors of office buildings throughout downtown St. Louis. Whatever it took, my father did his best to put food on the table. In doing so, he taught us to make sure our dollars made sense. To him, that meant embracing the old saying "A penny saved is a penny earned." During times of stress in life, he would often say, "Take care of business first, and cry later!" His attitude, along with my mother's insistence, "Be a now person; dare to be different!" strengthened me when others might have caved in and quit.

Education was a big deal for my mother. Although she married early and forsook her high school diploma and college degree, she valued knowledge and did everything to make sure we had a good education. In her opinion, the Catholics cornered the market on elementary education. Hence, I attended St. Rocks Catholic School from kindergarten through second grade. But my time there was cut short when my mother finally discovered on her own what I had been telling her all along, that the nuns weren't behaving very "nunly." They had split personalities it seemed. During a visit to the school, she witnessed for herself just what I had described—a nun vigorously spanking a child with a ruler. My mother would never allow anyone to mistreat us. The next day, we joined our neighborhood friends at the local elementary school.

As we grew older, my mother couldn't shield us from the inevitable—peer pressure. I withstood it all, though. At Big Hamilton Elementary School, my peers tried to get me to choose between smoking and their friendship. My dreams for the future gave me the confidence I needed to allow my destiny to override my physical surroundings. The visions of my dreams remained constant and full of great wonders. Some of my siblings, on the other hand, gave in. I saw their downward spiral firsthand. David, it seemed, caught the worst of it. Drugs and alcohol made him into sort of the black sheep of the family. He and his friends were in and out of different schools and jail for disturbing the peace. David's antics disturbed the peace not only in our community but also in our home. When David was twelve years old, doctors finally identified the reason for his behavior: he was diagnosed with schizophrenia and bipolar disorder. He drained so much time and energy from my parents and was the topic of most of our family meetings, so a lot of my childhood recollections are of him.

Many memories of my own upbringing are a blur. Yet I never

will forget a few near-death experiences that left permanent scars on my body. My siblings and I often contrived some pretty rough games. One day it was the guys against the girls. The next time, it could be the oldest four against the youngest four. One hot afternoon, the joke was on Alice and me. My brother told Alice I had played a practical joke on her. Exactly what I was accused of I never knew, nor was there time to find out. All that mattered in Alice's eyes was payback. Shoe in hand, she chased me all over the house. I ran from the kitchen through the living room, straight toward the light shining through the decorative glass on our front door. Like the North Star in the midnight sky, it signaled my path to freedom. Brows and hands sweaty from fear of Alice's threats and the imminent launch of her high-top tennis shoe, I reached for the doorknob. No luck. My hand slipped off the handle and broke through the glass panel. The momentum of my body slammed my shoulder into the sharp edges.

Back then, my family didn't go to the hospital unless it was absolutely necessary. I took one look at the ripped, gaping flesh on my wrist and shoulder and knew I would need more than my family's favorite "it-won't-hurt-if-you-don't-look" home remedy. The emergency room doctors stitched my wrist. I was one-half inch away from cutting my main artery.

Our family bicycle was called the Big Blue Bus. This huge, oversized bike was shared among the eight of us. One late afternoon, I had been waiting all day long for my turn to ride. Miss Alice leisurely rode down the street like she was an only child. As the streetlights started to flicker, my impatience turned to vengeance. I chased after her and jumped on the aluminum rack on top of the rear wheel, but the wheel caught me. My heel slid through the back spokes of the tire and became mangled as the wheels turned. Alice and I both began to cry: I was in pain, but she was in t-r-o-u-b-l-e! She carried me home as my foot dangled in distress. Again I needed stitches, but bills from the last emergency room inspired my father to apply his very own homemade "I'll-fix-it-myself" cure. He cleaned my wound, doctored my ripped heel back together, wrapped it tightly, and changed the bandage daily. As it healed, each stinging pain brought with it thoughts of purchasing my own bicycle.

After that experience, I made a mental note: sharing this one item among seven other people just doesn't work for me. When the temperature dropped and the autumn days grew shorter, an opportunity to get my own bike presented itself and I devised one of Halloween's greatest tricks and sweetest treats.

Hopping along on my mending foot, I managed to keep up with the trick-or-treaters. Throughout the night, I resisted the urge to indulge in the bartered bounty. My craving for the sweet sight of cash outweighed my desire for the sweet taste of my stash. In the days to come, my siblings and friends compared and consumed their Sugar Babies and Daddies, while my

Tootsie Rolls and Pops remained hidden within several shoe boxes beneath the bed I shared with Alice. After about a week, my siblings' and friends' candy was gone, and with it the steady flow of sugar through their veins. In need of a sweet fix, they were ripe to become customers at my makeshift storefront. My candy stash quickly turned into cash, and my inventory of hidden treasures reaped a 100 percent pure profit.

This seasonal boost combined with babysitting money soon gave me what I needed to purchase my first bicycle. I made my solo debut on a shiny chocolate, three-speed bike, whose color exemplified the sweet essence that made its purchase possible. Pride raced through my afro as I sped up and down the neighborhood. For years, I reopened my stash-to-cash store during the second week of November. Only Alice enjoyed my treats at a discounted rate. She and I were tight, and everyone knew it. We weren't just sisters; we were buddies. Although five years my senior, I was her shadow. When Alice participated in our neighborhood's song and dance group, I was her personal manager. When she snuck out for an evening of teenage frolicking and partying, I was her cover. We laughed at the same jokes, sang the same songs, and had each other's backs. Alice was a good role model for me. The mistakes I saw her make, I totally avoided. We were homemade, homegrown partners, total opposites, yet two of a kind.

∽

By my seventh birthday, my parents were separated. Since my mother became the breadwinner, my oldest sister, Sharon, took charge and became more like a second mother than a sibling to us. This arrangement meant that activities beyond the boundaries of our block were practically nonexistent. Then the Wilsons appeared. One Sunday morning, this white couple drove through our neighborhood and slowed down when they saw my friends and me playing. They stopped and invited us to Sunday school, promising ice cream afterwards. Why they chose the 5800 block of Pershing Avenue, only God knew. Fortunate for me, my mother was one of the parents who allowed her children to attend.

Sunday after Sunday, the Wilsons faithfully showed up and transported a growing number of children—and eventually parents—to church, followed by the promised dessert. The bait had hooked me. Without realizing it, through the lure of ice cream I strengthened my personal relationship with God. The Christian faith would be the foundation I needed for the rest of my life. Soon, three vehicles were needed, so the Wilsons invited their friend Diane Gilman to help escort us back and forth.

Wanting to free us from the confines of our immediate environment, the Wilsons and Mrs. Gilman came more frequently. They often took our neighborhood group to Forest Park Community College for swimming, to their homes, out to dinner, to the movies, and on other social outings. They also saw that we attended a summer Christian camp. Of course, I welcomed these adventures to expand my horizons and experience how life could be. My mother just didn't have the time or the funds to make it happen. Our newfound friends showed us a new version of the world, up close and personal. Before long, these encounters fueled my desire for more adventures and encouraged me to dream even bigger. My worldview expanded beyond the boundaries of Missouri and now surpassed the borders of the United States. Within me, an insatiable longing to visit other countries was birthed.

Lovell, a military man, fed my dreams with stories of his travels. He married my mother when I was fourteen and filled our home with enough humor to make us forget the pain of my parents' divorce. Lovell's serious side was reserved for Navy duties, which took him to sea six months at a time. His absence silenced our home, and we marked each day in anticipation of his arrival. When he returned, he filled my mind with exciting stories about different cultures and customs from around the world. I closed my eyes as he transported my sister Susan and me with his vivid descriptions of Alaska, the land of the midnight sun; the castles of Germany; the tropical island of Guam; the sandy beaches of Hawaii; the crowded cities in Japan; his shopping spree in Korea; the royalty of London; and the poverty in the Philippines. I knew that someday I too would travel to these exotic locations.

My daydreams of faraway places were often interrupted by the constant agony of my feet. The doctors diagnosed the steady pain as bunions and told my mother corrective surgery was needed. "Without surgery, walking will become too painful and running will only be a figment of her imagination," one doctor said. Not wanting the surgery, my mother and I prayed and believed corrective shoes would solve the problem. For at least two years I donned bright red shoes with braces that extended up both my legs to steer the bones in the right direction.

Alice was more embarrassed than I was at the sight of these shoes. One day while walking home, we took a shortcut through an alley. Alice stopped, once again blinded by the brightness of my therapeutic footwear.

"Girl, look, you can't even play hide-and-seek with those shiny red shoes. It's either you or those bright shoes of yours. One of you has got to go!" she proclaimed.

Since Alice was my girl, it was an easy choice for me. I trashed the shoes and walked out of that alley barefoot without a second thought.

"CHILE, WHERE YOUR SHOES AT?" my mother yelled when we arrived home.

Alice came to my rescue and cleverly changed the subject to distract Mother. We quickly disappeared out of our kitchen's back door to avoid disclosing the truth. By the time Mother asked again, the shoes had been hauled to the city dump, and she refused to buy me another pair.

When I reached high school, my mother determined our neighborhood schools had grown worse. She wanted Alice, Susan, and me out. With Mrs. Gilman's assistance, we applied to a Christian school about forty-five minutes from our home. Alice's was the only application rejected because she was already a senior, so she remained at the local high school. I don't know how my mother initially paid for us to attend this private school, but she soon figured out a way to make it work. She got a job as the switchboard operator at the school, which entitled us to receive the employee's tuition rate.

In the meantime, significant changes were taking place in our household. Sharon became friends with a man named Jim, who had plans to move to Seattle, Washington. A year later, they were married and soon had two sons. Over the years, one by one, most of my family migrated to Seattle as well. My birth father, Arthur, was first and then my older siblings—Vincent, Barron, Alice, and David (but not Kevin, who had joined the Army). Susan, the youngest, and I could only spend our summers visiting them so we could return home to St. Louis in the fall for school.

When I reached my sophomore year, however, Lovell was assigned to the Navy town of Bremerton, Washington, just an hour's drive or ferry ride from Seattle. Mother and Lovell moved immediately, but Susan and I finished the school year as boarders on our school's campus. When my parents decided the expense was too costly, they enrolled us in the local high school in Bremerton. There I ventured out to make the varsity track team. As a sprinter, I ran the 100-yard dash, the 220, and anchored the 440 relay. I also substituted for hurdles and long jumps. So much for doctors who once told me that without foot surgery running would be impossible!

After only one year in Bremerton, Lovell was relocated to Alameda, California. We moved to this Navy town for only six short months before we were relocated back to St. Louis. I had definitely earned my status as a military brat, but I decided to jump off this military roller coaster once I graduated. An academic scholarship to an accounting school in St. Louis helped.

As soon as I graduated, I too moved to Seattle. Much to my dismay, shortly after I arrived Alice's job transferred her from Seattle to Tacoma, Washington, forty-five minutes away. It didn't matter too much. Every weekend I closed the gap and drove to hang out with my sister. We were united once again as if never separated. I made back-to-back visits to Tacoma, a military town that was the home of Fort Lewis Army Base and McChord Air Force Base. Every Friday and Saturday night, Alice and I could be found at the local Non-Commissioned Officers' Club. In January 1982, Alice married a soldier in the U.S. Army. They were married only three days before he was sent away for a yearlong tour to Korea.

My accounting training reaped greater dividends when I landed a job working in the accounts receivable department of Grayline Tours Travel Agency in Seattle. I envied my bosses. They were paid to scout new vacation and honeymoon locations in places like the Bahamas, Hawaii, and Bermuda. They also sought out the best cruises and resorts and traveled to exotic destinations all over the world. Their visits ensured the accommodations were up to the company's standards. Getting paid to travel was my idea of a dream job. Every day on my way to work, I walked past downtown Seattle's Air Force recruiter's office. Hanging in their window was a sign that read, "Air Force Reserve—A Great Way to Serve." I agreed, recalling Lovell's traveling tales.

Lovell tried his best to encourage me to join the Navy, but there was no chance of that. I had to be first and foremost true to myself; I wasn't that fond of water. After much research, I discovered I liked the Air Force Reserve. During peacetime, reservists work one weekend a month and two weeks during the year. My decision was easy. I walked into the recruiter's office and told the sergeant I wanted to become an Air Force reservist and see the world! Within a month, I passed the military test, quit my job and moved in with Alice for two weeks before leaving for basic training at Lackland Air Force Base in Texas.

Even though basic training was fun and challenging, and I endured it pretty well, I wouldn't want to repeat it. The first week, my squadron was only given five minutes to eat. Many of my fellow airmen left the chow hall frustrated and hungry, but not me. Thanks to my large family, I was accustomed to eating quickly and often had time for seconds and dessert.

I survived basic training mostly by maintaining my sense of humor, because it was difficult to take some of the training instructors' commands seriously. One of the silly rules was that our underclothes had to be folded into six-inch lengths for inspections. Their mind games could either make or break you. You could choose to laugh or cry. I chose to laugh, which helped me meet even the most ridiculous demands.

I could deal with basic training and all of its military regimentation, but it was those hard-to-stretch, tight, low-quarter, leather-bound, unforgiving shiny black shoes that were no laughing matter. One evening when I took them off, I had blisters covering both feet. Early the next morning, I went to the doctor.

"Airman, do you know what you have?" he asked.

"No, sir," I responded.

"You have yourself a military discharge."

He told me he had just discharged five people for flat feet and that my blistered bunions were worse than their problem.

"If I had kept wearing those corrective shoes, I probably could have avoided this problem," I thought to myself.

There was no shame in my game. I begged the doctor not to

discharge me. The only reason he didn't return me to my civilian life was because I was a reservist and not on active duty status. I thanked God right then for His favor. The doctor issued me a straggler's pass, which excused me from running, jumping, and marching with my squadron. From then on, my feet became my trademark—I was the only airman sporting tennis shoes with my uniform, even while wearing my dress blues. Of course, this privilege came with constant inquiries and questioning.

During our dormitory inspections, everything had to be in its precise place. My squadron stood stiffly at attention as we nervously waited and watched one another's public humiliation. On the first day of wearing my new outfit, our training instructor saw my shoe display. As he stood in front of me, he yelled at the top of his lungs.

"AIRMAN TAYES, WHERE ARE YOUR LOW QUARTERS?"

In an instant, my mind flashed back to the day I left my bright red corrective shoes in the alley.

"CHILE, WHERE YOUR SHOES AT?" I could hear my mother yell.

Back then, Alice came to my rescue. This time, however, there was nowhere to escape. This man was all in my face.

"SIR, MY LOW QUARTERS ARE AT THE BRACE SHOP, SIR!" I responded loudly.

I was so embarrassed, but giving up wasn't a choice for me.

He just looked at me like I was pitiful and demanded to see my orders from the doctor.

Some people in my squadron couldn't handle the pressure. They were either put out or recycled (Air Force jargon for having to repeat the training), or they took the easy way out and just quit. Even then, the presence of the Lord assured me that being an Air Force reservist served an important purpose in my life's destiny and was my ticket to see the world, so I remained steadfast and held my ground. I was determined to succeed, and I did.

After I graduated from basic training, I attended an air cargo specialist school for another six weeks at Sheppard Air Force Base, Texas. There, I learned to drive forklifts, build pallets, and load and download air cargo planes. It was a far cry from working with numbers, but I enjoyed the change, challenge, and experience.

CHAPTER THREE

My "Lonely" Soldier

*"If you do not develop the hunger and courage to pursue your goal,
you will lose your nerve and you will give up on your dream."*

After basic training and technical school, I moved back to Tacoma, Washington, with Alice. Her husband was still on duty in Korea. One summer night, we went to the NCO Club. It was our usual hangout, as Alice always loved a good party. My return meant I assumed my usual role as her designated driver. That night, I went as is in my uniform of the day—blue jeans and tennis shoes, comfortable and easy.

For Washington, where summers are a mixture of coolness and rain, that evening was surprisingly perfect—warm with a clear, starlit sky. The NCO club was filled to capacity as usual. When we arrived, the dance floor was jam-packed, allowing us to grab a table, and we quickly sat down. Good timing. Across from us, we saw a handsome young man. In contrast to my casual jeans and tennis shoes, he was overdressed in black slacks and a nice, white, buttoned-up shirt. He sat alone; a look of solitude marked his face. When he looked our way, his glance became a stare, and he blatantly kept right on gazing.

Finally, he approached our table and asked Alice to dance. His goal, I later learned, was to meet me. Throughout the dance, he asked Alice about her companion and armed himself with sufficient information to approach me directly. Once the song ended, the lonely soldier returned to his seat, but Alice, always the cool, smooth dancer, stayed put on the floor and strutted in sync with the beat of the next song. I was again left alone, but only for a moment.

"Oh, the lonely soldier is headed my way. Here he comes!" As he walked toward me, I grew more and more nervous; I felt my heart skip a beat.

"Would you watch my drink?" he asked. "I have to go to the bathroom."

I started laughing out loud. I thought he would approach me with some smooth rehearsed line.

"Yes, I'll watch your drink for you," I somehow managed to say.

Upon his return, he thanked me and then asked me to dance. I accepted. Between dance moves, we attempted a conversation but couldn't contend with the loud music. However, hearing his voice jogged my memory. I remembered dancing with this man at the same club about four months before I left for basic training.

But things were different this time. As the song "Honey Wild" by Con Funk Shun ended, our romance began. We later coined the selection "our song." Together, we returned to his table and began exchanging bits of our lives.

It was a fun, meaningful conversation. His name was Surie. He bragged about the Army, and I about the Air Force. Having done active duty in the Army, he downplayed my experience in the Air Force's basic training as if it were summer camp. I shared my experience nonetheless, feeling proud of my recent accomplishment. My age was the next topic.

"Twenty years old," I told him when he asked. But he didn't believe me; I looked much younger. He asked to see identification, and when I showed him my military ID, he laughed when he realized I was two days older than him.

Before I knew it, like Cinderella, my time had ended before I was ready. The club was closing, and my duties resumed as Alice's chauffeur. Surie walked me to the car, where we exchanged phone numbers, and he invited me out the next day. I would have accepted if not for my military responsibilities. That night I wrote in my journal, "This could be something."

Despite the long night, the next day I managed to drag myself to McChord AFB for a full ten-hour workday. My lonely soldier called the instant I crossed the threshold of Alice's apartment at the end of the day. But the soldier didn't sound lonely anymore, nor was he thinking about being alone. In fact, he eagerly anticipated going out with me that evening.

"Alice and I are a package deal!" I told Surie.

I explained that as long as Alice's husband was overseas, I didn't feel comfortable leaving her behind. Alice, Surie, and I quickly became "The Three Musketeers," and the NCO club, our stage. This scene played time and time again because no mister was going to come between me and my sista! He didn't mind, especially since we all got along just fine.

Surie and I shared a lot in common and bonded like long-time best friends. Sounds like a cliché, I know, but for us it was true. Air Force versus Army comparisons and our closeness in age continued to be a running joke between us. For my twenty-first birthday, Alice and our friend Terri took me to a twenty-one-and-over club outside the base. There, I was christened an adult. I teased Surie, explaining that he couldn't join us because he was much too young and would have to wait outside the door way too long to get in.

After two months of dating and talking on the phone into the wee hours of the morning, cupid's arrow pierced our hearts, and we were in love. Even though I wasn't looking for a spouse, the thought of marriage had crossed my mind. This lonely soldier was fun to be around, generous, thoughtful, witty, and gainfully employed. Most importantly, he possessed the one quality I desired most in a spouse—humor.

Surie could make me laugh at the drop of a dime. He had the type of true comedic talent that I gravitated to. It reminded me of the humor Lovell brought to our family. Back then, I couldn't imagine spending my life with someone who couldn't bring the same joy to my life. Surie kept Alice and me laughing—a key that opened a place for him in our hearts. We welcomed him into our fold. More often than not, you wouldn't see just two us, but all three.

That was before my dreams were completely deflated. One night after a dinner date, Surie became strangely uncomfortable and began talking in circles. Finally, he stammered under his breath, "I'm m-m-m-married, m-married."

"Oh Lord! Good God. Player, player!" I screamed inside. "You cut me deep. What betrayal!" I couldn't believe it. How could this happen to cautious me? Angela, "The Seventh Wonder" wondering, what now? Me, a mistress! A home wrecker! Caught up in a love triangle. I was through. Another woman—rightfully—sported the wedding band of the man I had come to claim as mine. If I had only known, but that was just it; I didn't. My perception was influenced by deception.

I was right in thinking Surie was good husband material, but legally he wasn't available. My womanly intuitions failed me this time. I learned firsthand that everything that glitters isn't gold. But how could I have been so naive? I wasn't sure where to place the blame—on my gullibility or Surie's cleverness.

Everywhere Surie and I went, whether to the mall, clubs, movies, or just around the base, he treated me like I was the only lady in his life. And I believed him. He never gave me a reason to think otherwise. His friends were so programmed, they continued the lie well after the truth was revealed.

I'm not sure how long the cover-up would have continued if Surie had not planned a trip to his hometown, Miami, where his wife, from whom he was separated, lived. Two days before he left, guilt must have forced his confession. What hurt most was that on the night we met, I specifically and directly asked Surie if he was married because he wore a ring on his wedding finger.

"No, it's a military ring, and this is the only finger it fits," he assured me.

I examined it. It was a military ring, as he had stated, but I know now that it replaced his wedding band. His game would have worked; his mistake was he had grown in love with this Seventh Wonder.

Surie and his wife hadn't been married a year when the union was threatened. His deep-seated belief that the marriage was doomed from the start supposedly justified his actions. He married in a rushed, hushed, and unsober state of mind. He didn't have the heart to cancel after she had notified guests and rented the hall.

The week that Surie was home in Miami he called frequently, attempting to allay the hurt and anger that surfaced in every question screaming from me.

"How dare you lie to me!" I yelled. "I thought we were honest with one another!"

Like a batter hitting balls from home plate, he knocked my concerns out of the ballpark one by one. I didn't want to hear it. I was mad at him and at myself for falling in love with a married man. I wished I could have just turned my feelings off, but my heart was not in accord with my head. Each response, professing his allegiance to our relationship, nudged at my emotions.

When he left for Miami he had one suitcase. Upon his return there were three. "Are those extra bags your wife's luggage?" I asked at the airport.

"No, these belong to someone more important than she'll ever be to me," he answered.

Unless his mother was coming, I knew he was referring to a child. I prepared for more heart-wrenching news. I was right. He and his wife were new parents of a son, which was the reason for his home visit. He explained that they would be coming to Washington next month after he completed a two-week field duty exercise with his unit.

Learning about Surie's son and upcoming reunion unleashed another river of tears. With this much drama, my life was beginning to look like an episode from the *Jenny Jones Show*.

"Sister girl, drop that zero for a hero!" I could hear the show's audience advise me. Of course those words are much easier said than done when it's not your heart that's involved.

The next time I saw Surie, I asked to see pictures of his wedding. Because he had done such a good job of hiding his marriage, it was still hard for me to believe it was true. Reality hit, nonetheless, as each photo solidified the truth. Emotionally, I was exhausted.

Alice learned of Surie's betrayal from a distance—literally. Before the start of a speech class in which the two of us were enrolled, I slipped her one of the wedding pictures and then quickly took my seat on the opposite side of the room. As disgusted as I was over the whole matter, I couldn't help but laugh as I watched Alice's eyes fixate on the photograph.

She couldn't pay any attention to the teacher. Instead, she sat there on pins and needles, as the picture had provoked a boatload of questions. She tried to get students to pass me notes, but I ignored them. She attempted to get us sent to the administration office. I wouldn't go. She asked the teacher if the class could take an emergency break. The answer was no. Finally after class, Alice demanded answers. She had hoped the picture was trick photography or some sort of practical joke, but unfortunately the picture spoke a thousand words by revealing the truth.

That same evening, Alice let Surie have it, leaving no syllable unturned as she tore into him, giving him the third, fourth, and fifth degree up one aisle and down the other. I was surprised the man endured it.

"How dare you lead my sister on, married while fronting like a single man!" "What are your intentions?" "Why is your wife coming back if you're leaving her?" she demanded to know.

As the questions went on and on, believe it or not, I actually felt sorry for Surie, even though Alice embodied the rage within my heart. With every fiber of her being, Alice expressed her anger over his violation of my heart.

Surie did what he knew he must—apologize profusely, accept full responsibility, and explain his actions. His story was simple. The lie, he said, was necessary because he wanted to get to know me. He was right to think I would never have gotten involved with a married man.

"We don't want to hear all of your lies and fake apologies," Alice stated firmly.

"I need to ask my wife for a divorce and forgiveness face-to-face," he explained.

That gesture alone may have been his saving grace because it showed his character more than any expressions of regret. A true player would never care about his victim's feelings, but instead would cowardly cut ties three thousand miles away. I should have known from his opening line that he wasn't a player.

I was hurt, and I let Surie know how I felt. "I would never allow myself to knowingly be used or to play second fiddle to anyone for any reason," I told him.

My struggling heart might shake, bake, ache, then break, but I refused to be one of those females who puts her life on hold for months or years while her supposed man is waiting for the perfect time to tell his wife. I knew that with or without me in his life, his marriage was in jeopardy. Though I never gave him an ultimatum, I explained I would not continue our relationship while he was married.

Surie's wife came to Washington as planned, carrying more than just her luggage and their child. Rightfully so, she had heavy chips on both shoulders. Her friend had already told her that Surie was dating someone, and he didn't deny it.

After the fifth day of no contact, Surie called from work around 2 a.m. He told me he was moving forward with his divorce and that his wife would be leaving at the end of the month.

"Think it through and be able to live with your choices," I said. "No matter what, your son needs his father."

Because Surie wanted to do the right thing, his decision to divorce wasn't easy for him. Before dawn on Thanksgiving morning, Surie called and asked if he was still invited for dinner.

"You're not going to spend the day with your family?" I asked, puzzled.

"Angela, Sergeant Daniel took them to the airport. They're on a plane headed to Miami."

I'm not proud, but truth be told, news of her departure put my heart at ease, and, once again, I anticipated spending my life with the man I truly loved.

The Lord had mercy on Surie and me. At the time, I didn't know about the sanctity of the marriage covenant. I had never experienced a situation such as this, and I simply didn't understand or identify with the pain our relationship inflicted on his wife and child. Back then, I justified my actions by telling myself I didn't know Surie was married. It's amazing the stupid things we do when we're young and in love. Surie and I both came from broken homes, but that's no excuse for being out of order. We repented for our actions, and God tossed our misdeeds into the sea of forgiveness and forgetfulness. We too have learned to do the same. In His grace, God watches over His children, even the foolish ones.

CHAPTER FOUR

IN SICKNESS AND IN HEALTH

"If you're casual about your dreams,
they will end up as casualties."

Surie asked my father, Arthur, and my stepfather, Lovell, for my hand in marriage.

"Marry quickly before the obvious love potion wears off," Lovell the comedian said.

Lovell's counsel conflicted with Clara's advice to move slowly. Clara, Surie's sister, was right, but Surie's new set of military orders to Germany affected our decision to wait. Alice's husband returned from overseas as Surie and I were making our plans to leave. Surie relocated. A few months later, I informed my commander I would be leaving the country and was placed on inactive duty status with the Air Force.

German marriage laws would have delayed our wedding for at least another six months, so after the completion of Surie's divorce, we boarded the "wedding train" to Vejle, Denmark, and married in July of 1984. The city of Vejle, known as Darling Denmark, featured quick and easy marriages by the Danish justice of the peace. In Denmark, you had to be a citizen to get married, which only took three days. Many couples preferred this time frame over having to wait.

At the courthouse, there were about ten couples ahead of us waiting to get married. After each set of "I do's," it was customary for the minister and each newly wedded couple to take a shot of liquor. They should have rotated ministers, because by the time it was our turn, the minister was a little tipsy and could hardly complete a sentence clearly. We had trouble understanding him and figured his pauses signaled it was time to say our "I do's."

Starting our marriage overseas may have been the best place to begin. In Germany, we couldn't make or receive collect telephone calls or easily run home to our families in the face of problems. Under these conditions, relationships either briskly break or strongly strengthen. The latter described ours: we grew together, learning to live and love as one.

After a year of marriage, Surie and I were expecting our first child. We were so thrilled and excitedly began making all sorts of plans. I wanted a girl, he a boy. With assistance from friends who were already parents, I was preparing to be the best mother I could be. When Surie's field duty took him away from the base in Aschaffenburg for two and three days at a time, I often visited my friend Jay Hall, who helped me get ready for our new addition. One day, while deeply engaged in baby talk at Jay's home, I suddenly felt ill and decided to go home. She lived within walking distance of my apartment. I became dizzier with every step. I felt I was going to faint, and the chill November breeze wasn't enough to cool me down. When I made it home to my apartment, three flights of stairs greeted me. Very slowly I struggled with each step. Once inside, I removed a few layers of clothes, lay down and went right to sleep. Hours later I awoke, went to the bathroom and miscarried my baby.

Physically I felt a whole lot better, but spiritually I didn't understand why my pregnancy ended so abruptly. I had just spent over ten weeks sharing my body and mind with my child and then suddenly, prematurely, we were separated forever. I felt overwhelming emptiness. I cried uncontrollably, and then my thoughts quickly raced to Surie, who was due home the next day from field duty. How would he take the sad news?

When I told Surie about the miscarriage, he could hardly believe it. He didn't want to believe it, and he had lots of questions. He wondered how he would cope now that our baby was suddenly gone. He even blamed himself, thinking that God was punishing him for his divorce, but we know God forgives and forgets. He especially struggled with not being with me at the time I miscarried. We held each other tighter than ever before, silently letting reality set in. I knew that just as my presence had dispelled Surie's loneliness the night we met in that crowded NCO Club, his presence now eased my emptiness.

∽

Thanksgiving and Christmas drew near and a second year had almost passed without Surie taking a vacation. He requested leave the week of Christmas 1985. However, rank does have its privileges, and with others above him, the answer was no. Surie was granted the first week of December instead. I wanted to join him at home, but I was being trained for a new position at my accounting job.

I was only at work about an hour when I received a strange call. The voice on the other end of the line muttered something, but the person's speech was so slurred that I couldn't understand the words or even recognize the voice. Then I heard a dial tone. The call had disconnected. I tried to refocus on my work, but my spirit was unsettled. All of a sudden, I couldn't get the numbers to add up correctly. My mind was still distracted from the unusual call. I wondered if that unrecognizable voice could have been Surie pretending to be sick so I would join him. What would I do with this comedian during his two weeks of leave? I called home to check and to confirm our lunch date.

When I dialed my telephone number, the same incoherent voice from the earlier call tried to say something and then hung up. I still didn't recognize the voice or understand the words, but I knew I had called my home. Whether I informed my boss that I left, I can't recall since I sped right home. When I got there, my husband, in a cold sweat, was outside attempting to walk six blocks to the dispensary. I saw his distress and rushed him there. He managed to communicate that his head hurt terribly. His words were nearly incomprehensible. This was no joke; Surie was in trouble.

The physicians' assistants looked Surie over and asked a few questions. Because of his slurred speech and current leave status, they immediately assumed his symptoms were due to drugs or alcohol abuse. Instantly, they tested for contraband, checked for needle marks all over his body, and demanded I tell them what drugs he had consumed.

"He's not on any drugs!" I screamed.

"Protecting your husband could cause his health situation to become worse," one physician's assistant responded.

So convinced of their visual diagnosis, they practically initiated my husband's dishonorable discharge right then and there. They were dumbfounded when the drug test results proved his innocence and swiftly changed the "diagnosis" to a migraine headache. Their opinion was strong when wrong, but they were weak when it came to being right. All they could come up with to treat him were three shots—one in his arm and two in his behind—and another two hours of observation. Then they sent us home.

All night, I kept cool towels on Surie's head, trying to break the cold sweat that persisted throughout the night. At 6 a.m., I demanded we return to the dispensary, but he didn't want to go through more questions or poking. I tried to change his sweat-soaked shirt. By that time, his head hurt so badly he wouldn't let me touch him.

As his condition grew worse, my thoughts did too. I thought about his family in Florida, whom I hadn't met yet. If Surie died, what would I tell his mother? So, stanky shirt and all, with all of his weight leaning on me, we made it down our stairwell, to the car, and back to the dispensary. I wasn't about to lose him.

"What are they doing back here?" I overheard one of the physicians' assistants say to his co-worker. "I gave him enough drugs to knock a horse out."

"Look, I don't know what you gave my husband, but he's in serious pain," I told them.

They put Surie on a gurney, rolled him into a small exam room, closed the door behind us, and came in every now and then. I became really upset because Surie's speech was getting worse by the minute. I left the secluded room in search of any doctor in any position. The situation demanded that my polite patience turn to assertiveness.

"It's obvious you can't or won't do anything for my husband. If you're not going to get an ambulance to take him to the military hospital in Frankfurt, I will take him there myself!" I yelled.

Lord knows I didn't know how to get there, but I refused to just sit any longer and watch my husband deteriorate. Once more, they told me to sit still and wait, so I had to get ugly. I stopped reasoning and making concessions and started taking names of all whom I deemed guilty so I could file a report. The physicians' assistants and staff hadn't seen this side of me, and neither had I. I grabbed the telephone and called First Sergeant Jackson and the base commander. It wasn't until then that the medical staff showed Surie and I the respect and service we deserved. Within minutes after my call, an ambulance came to transport my husband to the military hospital in Frankfurt.

The doctors in Frankfurt were much more professional and knowledgeable.

"Sergeant Alexander, where is the pain?" one of the doctors asked.

Surie pointed to the left side of his head and muttered, "Ains."

Puzzled, the doctors and I looked at one another, hoping someone could decipher his speech.

"Baby, did you say AIDS?" I asked Surie. "Because if he said AIDS, forget about him and come check me out!" I told the doctors. Everyone laughed, but I was serious.

A little more clearly this time, Surie managed to pronounce the *p* and said "Pain."

The doctors shined their flashlight in Surie's eyes, checked his vitals signs, and ordered a CAT scan (Computer Aided Tomography) of his head right away. Three hours later, the results from the scan moved everyone to urgency.

"Your husband has a blood clot bleeding into his brain. We're flying you both to Landstuhl, Germany, for immediate brain surgery," a doctor quickly told me.

He continued talking, but I walked out of the room. Surie's diagnosis had gone from drug abuse to a severe migraine headache to brain surgery all within a twenty-four-hour time span. It was a bit much for me to take in so suddenly.

Immediately, Surie was being prepared for surgery. A helicopter came quickly, and within minutes we were off the ground. While in the air, the doctors on the flight were in communication with the neurosurgeon at Landstuhl Medical Center. From Surie's symptoms alone, Dr. Klara, the neurologist, diagnosed the problem as a brain aneurysm. Once we landed in Landstuhl, he explained the necessity of first performing an angiogram before rushing into surgery.

"The results of this test will tell us the exact location, size, and severity of the blood clot that caused the aneurysm," the doctor said.

When the results were in, Dr. Klara sat down and held my hand very tightly. "Surie was born with a weak blood vessel, which has erupted. This is the worst aneurysm I have ever seen in my entire career. The blood clot is bleeding in the part of the brain that controls his speech. That's why Surie's words were immediately incomprehensible," he explained to me.

Surie was moved to the surgical intensive care unit, and Dr. Klara arranged for me to stay in a guesthouse on base. The next day, December 3, I sensed that Dr. Klara had begun sugar-coating Surie's condition and I asked that he give it to me straight. When he did, his words were real and to the point.

"You'll probably be a widow by Christmas," Dr. Klara admitted.

The thought of Surie's condition being fatal caused my knees to buckle and my eyes to fill with tears. All of a sudden I felt alone. Quickly, the German signs, language, and sounds around me, which I had eagerly adapted to, became increasingly unfamiliar. Miles from my family and home, I realized I had no support system here. It was the same feeling I had when I miscarried the month before—empty inside.

While sitting in the waiting room, I thought about how my miscarriage afforded me the necessary energy for this crisis. If I had been pregnant, I would have been almost four months along. The stress from Surie's ordeal would probably have put me on bed rest at a time when my husband's life was at stake and he needed me most.

Immediately, I connected with everything I'd been taught about faith and God's healing power. I took control of my emotions, refused to accept the doctor's prediction and prayed for a victorious outcome.

"I might be a widow by Christmas, but not the Christmas of nineteen hundred and eighty-five," I said to myself.

I took a moment, replayed the events leading up to this present time and realized that it could have been much worse. The morning of the aneurysm, Surie ordinarily would have been running as part of his daily military physical training. Thank God he was on leave and at home in bed resting. If not, they might have called me from the morgue because he could have died in his tracks.

A few close friends from Aschaffenburg drove in for moral support once they heard about the situation. Their presence and comfort helped strengthen me for the next round.

"We don't have the people or the technology to perform the surgery in Germany, so Surie will have to be flown to Walter Reed Army Medical Center in Washington, D.C., for his surgery," Dr. Klara shared with us.

"Our first task is to get him there. In order to handle the altitude, distance, and cabin pressure of the flight, Surie's brain needs to be relieved of its pressure, which will take about two weeks."

Despite Surie's stable condition, Dr. Klara prepared for the worst and asked if there was anyone Surie would want to see before we left for the Walter Reed Hospital. My brother Kevin and Sergeant Daniel, Surie's long-time military friend, were stationed in Germany, so I asked them to come. Surie would enjoy their visit, and I needed all four of their strong shoulders to lean on. Immediately, their commanders placed them on emergency leave, and they arrived the next day.

During this time, Surie received permanent change of station orders. Everything, from returning my library books and finding a home for our fish to shipping our furniture and car back to the United States, needed to be done yesterday. Landstuhl was three hours away from Aschaffenburg. First Sergeant Jackson assigned a personal driver to escort me back and forth. I didn't eat or sleep much; I just prayed and checked off my to-do list. Despite my efforts, I knew I had lost it the day I stood in front of the ATM machine on base and could not recall my PIN number. I sat on the stairs of the bank for over an hour and just let the much-needed time escape. I don't know why, but out of all the major decisions I was making, forgetting my PIN number broke me down.

Dr. Klara knew the severity of Surie's condition and admitted he didn't know what was keeping Surie alive. It was hard at times for me to accept the seriousness of his brain aneurysm because Surie was in such a good mood, and when he tried to communicate, his impaired speech sounded so funny. I knew Surie didn't fully grasp the gravity of his condition even though he was told. His thoughts and conversations were of returning to the field with his troops. In fact, Surie's chattiness resulted in a gag order from his doctors, who wanted his brain to remain calm.

Dr. Klara privately shared with me that he had witnessed many couples separate over medical conditions that weren't nearly as serious as Surie's illness. He blatantly asked me not to leave my husband—a thought that had never even entered my mind.

On medical planes, patients are normally attended to by the nurses. In our case, Dr. Klara personally escorted us to Walter Reed. He was so concerned Surie wouldn't survive the flight that he didn't delegate this responsibility. Dr. Klara sat right next to me on the plane, medical bag in hand, closely monitoring Surie's condition as he slept. Dr. Klara couldn't explain Surie's endurance, but I knew it was the grace of God.

"If Surie survives the surgery, he will never again be the man you married, and the military will permanently retire him," he told me.

My brain overloaded. I gazed at Dr. Klara and nodded upon hearing this information. Now it was me who was unable to grasp the full meaning of the situation. Surie had been in the Army for seven years and had planned to stay in for at least another twenty. He was a dedicated soldier in every sense of the word.

At Walter Reed Hospital, Surie was labeled their miracle patient for enduring and surviving the fourteen-hour flight from Germany. In the waiting room, I met my in-laws for the first time. Clara had come from Miami with her daughter, Kaysheila, and

Surie's two-year-old son. Surie's three sisters were there: Paulette from New Jersey; Willie May, a nurse from North Carolina, and her three children; and Lizzie, a speech pathologist, who lived just fifteen minutes from the hospital. Surie's mother, Precious, also a nurse; her husband, Joe; and their three children had also come. (Surie's father, Surie Sr., had passed in 1979.) Surie's family asked all the right medical questions, and their support made it easier for me to decipher the doctor's recommendations for my husband's medical procedures. The doctors told us he would need two surgeries, but they were concerned about possible complications—he could be paralyzed, suffer amnesia, behave violently afterward, or even die.

Lizzie invited me to live with her during this time. Clara joined me at the hospital the morning of the first surgery. Before dawn, we arrived to pray over Surie and the doctor's hands. The surgery lasted over eighteen hours. Early the next morning, Surie awakened from the anesthesia.

"I love you. You're beautiful. Give me kisses," Surie repeated, no matter what questions were asked of him or by whom. I was just thankful he had something to say! But that didn't last for long. The next day his brain began to swell from the operation, and he couldn't speak at all.

The doctors had already warned us to expect the worst, but I thought surely after they repaired the blood clot we would be able to understand his speech. Surie's conversation showed no improvement and got a whole lot worse before it began to get better. I was extremely thankful he didn't wake up behaving violently or suffer from any paralysis, but I wanted my prayers answered immediately. We are taught to accept that our prayers are answered before we see the outcome, but it would have been just phenomenal to name it and instantly claim it, confess it and possess it, believe it and receive it, blab it and grab it in the flesh right here and now—you know, that supernatural but actual healing that only our Maker can deliver. But nooooo. Seriously, since then I've realized there were other lessons I needed to learn and levels of trust and faith that I could only achieve by going through the journey.

While we were trying to figure out what Surie was saying, Alice walked into the room. Surie was so excited to see her. He tried to say "The Three Musketeers" and hold up our three-finger signal, but five fingers were displayed instead. Lizzie advised us from the very beginning that we could either laugh or cry. We chose to laugh. Alice stayed with us for two weeks as we planned for our homecoming after Surie's release from the hospital.

During the surgery, the left side of Surie's skull was detached for the majority of the operation. The skull was kept in a sterile environment; the doctors didn't want to chance any infections. Dr. George told me he had seen a patient's head swell beyond recognition from contamination by a speck of dust. Three months later, Surie had another five-hour surgery to replace a portion of his skull with a mold. Clara again accompanied me, offering not only her presence but also her prayers.

While in the waiting room, Clara explained that now that she thought about it, Surie's aneurysm was likely the cause of some of her brother's weird childhood behaviors. Customarily, Surie would come home from school and head straight for the refrigerator. One day he went directly to his bedroom, stripped down to his underwear, and ran out the front door. Clara chased him, but Surie was quick. Luckily, a group of guys playing football down the street tackled him and brought him home. Concerned, Clara took Surie to the hospital, where a series of tests were conducted, including a drug test. Unfortunately, the results failed to explain Surie's strange behavior that day. When Surie came to himself, he didn't remember anything about flashing or dashing.

After Surie awakened from the second surgery, his speech remained indecipherable. Communicating through writing was also hindered because he couldn't remember the alphabet. Thank God Lizzie was a speech pathologist and began giving Surie her own brand of "How Now, Brown Cow" therapy. Those sessions were so hilarious, each could have been recorded and sold for comic relief. When asked to touch his ear, Surie touched his nose. When asked to touch his toes, he touched his elbows. The funny thing was that Surie responded confidently, as if to say, "All right, I did that. Bring it on. What's next? That's all you women got?" Paulette and I were behind the door on the floor hollering. Humor heals, so we were grateful that Surie's funny bone was still intact. Otherwise this time could have been very depressing for us all.

People often ask me how I coped hour after hour through both surgeries. The truth is, I felt calm realizing just how far God had already brought us. To think that Surie and I had spent any time disappointed about his request for vacation during Christmas week! We simply weren't aware that the denial was God's early Christmas miracle that likely spared his life.

The miracles continued. After eight months, the doctors released my husband from Walter Reed Hospital. Surie suffered memory loss and speech impairment, but not as severe as had been predicted. He was discharged from the military. The problem was that he felt he was kicked out of the Army— this was his life. The blessing was that his honorable medical discharge granted him full retirement benefits.

∽

At home in Washington, recovery was slow. Surie was childlike and copied me. When I ate, he ate. When I combed my hair, he tried too. The problem was, he was bald. Although he knew we were married and who his relatives were, he got the relationships all mixed up. He improperly identified aunts and uncles, in-laws and cousins, and he introduced me as his husband all the time. Pronouns were extremely difficult for him. Dr. George confirmed that Surie was aware of the correct names and pronouns, but explained that the information scrambled in his head by the time he spoke. A funny example of this was the day a solicitor came to our home to sell encyclopedias and Surie answered the door.

"Can I speak to the lady of the house?" asked the salesman.

"I am the lady of the house," Surie answered.

Awestruck, the salesman glared at Surie, slowly backed up, and left the block. I witnessed the whole scene from my perch on the stairwell and couldn't stop laughing. My husband stood astonished and questioned what had just happened. He truly didn't know, so I repeated the scenario. He insisted he never uttered that response.

"Listen, I got my brain fixed—you didn't. What I had might be contagious. I'm concerned for you. Get Doctor George on the phone. You really need to make an appointment today," he struggled to say.

Such confusion occurred frequently in our home, so much so that I began questioning my own sanity. But his "new brain" had few explanations for mail placed in the refrigerator, garden tools in the laundry room, and groceries all over the house. We needed to have a child—I needed a witness in our home.

Most of our time was spent going from speech to physical to occupational therapy sessions. Then the seizures began. For this I wasn't prepared. Even though Surie had been on seizure medication, it wasn't until eight months after his release from the hospital that he experienced his first episode. It happened on a visit to my father's house. Surie didn't get out of the car right away.

"I'll be out in a minute," he insisted.

"Okay," I said.

I got out, shut my door, and went inside. After a couple of minutes, I returned to the car to find Surie glaring at me through the window. When he began to shake uncontrollably, I yelled his name and fumbled with my car keys in a panic. Family members rushed to my screams. Finally, I got the car door open and we removed Surie from the car and laid him on the grass. Instinctively, my father used his comb to hold down Surie's tongue. Though the grand mal seizure lasted less than a minute, it seemed much longer. It scared all of us. I'm so glad I wasn't alone. For several years, Surie continued having seizures about every five to six months. Each time, the doctors adjusted his medication.

As time passed, I became so consumed with Surie's medical condition that my desires and dreams of seeing the world escaped me. In an effort to find myself again, I arranged for a shuttle to transport Surie to and from his therapy sessions. This alone time while he was away felt awkward to me. I didn't know what to do with myself. Caring for Surie had become my life. Resuming duties in the Air Force Reserves was the answer. It offered me the chance to focus my energy, at least partly, on something besides being a caregiver. Alice agreed to help with Surie whenever my military commitments took me away on weekend duties and annual tours.

Now retired, Surie felt lost too. When your retirement is planned, it can be a wonderful experience. But it's frustrating when you're young and your health prevents you from working. Suddenly, you have all this time on your hands without the freedom or independence to enjoy it. Surie was accustomed to the Army's way of life, where you do more before six in the morning than most people do all day. He just wanted to change places with me each time I put my uniform on. Yet, at the same time, you could tell he was proud of me as he shined my boots for me.

CHAPTER FIVE

LIFE WORTH CELEBRATING

"You cannot expect to achieve new goals or move beyond your present circumstances unless you change."

In some ways, my life seemed to mirror Alice's. She and I both married military men. In 1987, she delivered a stillborn child, and I miscarried for a second time. But when Alice became pregnant again, I got excited. Five months into her pregnancy I too was expecting, and soon we both delivered healthy baby girls. I planned to name my daughter Alicia after Alice, but when she named her daughter Lareina Alicia, I named my daughter after myself as well.

By the time Lareina turned two months, Alice was with child again. That's right. She was pregnant again and had a baby boy she named Arsenio. Arsenio was born eleven months to the day after Lareina's birthday. Again, I got excited. I knew I would have a second child and my child would be a boy too. Does history repeat itself, or do people repeat history?

One Friday, Surie and I had lunch at a soul food restaurant at the Freighthouse Square, an indoor market with lots of retail shops and restaurants. At that time, I was seven months pregnant with our son Murice, and we had just received a good report from the doctor. Positioned in the heart of downtown Tacoma, Freighthouse Square draws a busy working and weekend crowd.

"This place still needs a balloon shop," said Sonny, the owner, right out of the blue as we ate our lunch. Sonny went on to explain that his family originally intended to open a balloon shop, but they chose to go into the food business instead.

"Why don't you open one?" he asked us.

"This man is crazy! He doesn't even know us," I whispered to Surie.

"The only balloon I'm looking forward to popping is the water sac surrounding my baby," I told Sonny.

Surie and I continued our meal and conversation and didn't give his suggestion another thought. Later, I jokingly mentioned the conversation to Alice, but she didn't find one ounce of humor in it. Instead, she saw an opportunity and insisted I drive her to the location. We ran into the manager, who showed us several available retail spaces. By evening's end, I was sold on her enthusiasm and found myself co-signing the lease. She had cleverly convinced me that we could do this. Her conviction told me we would do this. And thanks to an insurance settlement

Alice and I had just received from a guy who hit us while we were stopped at a red light, we did do this.

Sure, we should have done a market analysis, prepared a financial plan, written a mission statement, and signed a partnership agreement between the two of us, but we knew our sisterhood was more than enough. Our "business plan" was short, sweet, and to the point. How hard could it be to blow up a balloon? Now, for you aspiring entrepreneurs, I don't recommend starting a business this way. This is just the way it unfolded for Alice and me. Nor do I recommend the extreme opposite, which is analysis paralysis.

Looking back, I'm glad we moved so fast because fear never had a chance to catch up to us. In fact, it was quite the opposite. We hit the ground running. First we ran to the competition, a balloon shop located just two blocks down from the Freighthouse Square. We needed inventory and purchased our supplies from them at wholesale prices. We even invited our competitors to our grand opening.

Alice and I were good business partners. We thought alike and had the same goals. The older we grew, the less significant was the five-year age difference between us. With that said, we still had our days. But as the saying goes, "If two people always agree, then one of them isn't needed." And, boy, did we need one another. Alice was full of ideas and creativity, and I the fortitude and grounding to bring them to fruition. Entrepreneurship was in our bloodline.

One issue, however, required an outside player, a neutral party, a voice of reason. In the planning stages of our business, Alice rushed into the shop one day and told me she wanted to change the name we had originally agreed upon—Balloony Tunes—to 1313 Balloony Tune Lane.

"What? Where did you get that name from?" I asked. Knowing my sister's humorous personality, I knew there had to be a good story behind this, so I sat down for the full explanation.

"You know my favorite television show is *The Munsters*, second to *I Love Lucy*," she began.

Through my laughter, I managed to respond, "Yes, I know this."

"Well, the Munsters' home address is 1313 Mockingbird Lane," she managed to say with a straight face.

After I picked myself up off the floor, we went through some touchy negotiations, because Alice was quite serious about this. We consulted a friend, who helped put this fire out. I just couldn't see naming our business 1313 Balloony Tune Lane. In the name of sound business and partnership, we compromised and agreed on Ba'Loonnie Toone Lane.

Ba'Loonnie Toone Lane made its debut in November 1990 with a marvelous grand opening. The name of our store brought out the comedians. With Lane at the end, practical jokers often called and asked if they could reserve a lane for bowling.

"Yes, your lane will be ready by eight o'clock. Come early

and stay late" was always our response. We closed our shop at six, so we always felt we got the last laugh.

As it turned out, the very same week we opened for business, my Air Force Reserve unit was activated overseas for a six-month tour as part of Operation Desert Shield and Operation Desert Storm. Notified on a Tuesday, my unit was scheduled to depart that Thursday. Thankfully, my pregnancy with Murice disqualified me for deployment. Instead, until I delivered, they assigned me to the administrative office at McChord AFB, twenty minutes from my home. Murice kept me stateside at a time when our business and family needed me. For this reason, we called him our miracle child.

Nonetheless, the Persian Gulf War almost put a pin in our balloon business. In order to avoid going out of business the same week we opened, Alice was forced to carry the majority of the workload while I carried my baby and served our country. At the end of my day, all I could do was go home, put my feet up, and call Alice to discuss the day's business. I was only able to offer my advice and moral support. Through it all, Alice was so optimistic.

"I don't know about tomorrow, but today we're okay," she would say. We learned the value of taking one day at a time. Anything else would have been too overwhelming.

During my last trimester, there was talk of extending my unit for another six months. On May 2, 1991, Murice was born, two years after my daughter, Angela. Their births filled our hearts with the joy of parenthood. At last I had two much-needed witnesses in the house.

Once I cleared my postnatal, six-week medical evaluation, the Air Force expected me to join my unit in Germany. Simply stated, an extended overseas tour away from my family and the business was on the horizon. My orders were cut and the ink was drying fast. Again, God's amazing grace intervened: just one week before I was due to leave, another unit rotated in our stead and I was spared from leaving. My unit returned to reserve status, and I resumed my daily work at the balloon shop, where business was booming.

By the third month of business, customers wanted more than just balloons; they also wanted clowns. We were keeping the clowns in our Rolodex very busy. So after watching that money walk out the front door one too many times, crazy Alice decided to go to clown school. There she met Marvin Hardy, the class instructor. He also offered his students on-the-job balloon sculpturing lessons. I joined Alice in taking advantage of this opportunity and soon discovered that in the balloon industry, Marvin was "the man."

Our one-sentence business plan signaled to Marvin that he needed to take us under his wing if our shop was to survive. Within six months, we reaped the benefits of Marvin's tutelage, and balloons weren't the only thing expanding each day.

Through sculpturing, we learned to transform a room into a magical event. Marvin's mentorship taught us the dynamics of balloon artistry and gave us the knowledge we needed to take our business to a whole new level. It opened doors to a world of opportunities we hadn't even considered.

As our business statement developed into a descriptive business plan, our services expanded and our efforts were quickly met with increasing demand. After a few years, we outgrew the Freighthouse Square and moved to a larger location on 72nd Street in Tacoma, Washington.

During this time, teaching our babies to talk turned out to be just as beneficial for them as it was for Surie. It helped him match his speech with his cognitive awareness, which meant he could now identify objects and people with more accuracy. Unintentionally, Surie became a student. Things began lining up nicely.

After six years of therapy and much prayer, Surie regained his independence, and normalcy returned to our household. It became rare for him to refer to me as his husband or our children as his siblings, and he began placing items in their proper place. I was no longer his caregiver, and Surie embraced fatherhood with the vigor his renewed health allowed. The doctors finally found the right combination of medication to control his seizures, and with driver's rehabilitation classes, Surie earned back his driving privileges. He was so happy; he now treasured something he had once taken for granted.

Between our families and the business, Alice and I had our hands full. We both toiled away to make it all work, but the pressure became too much. Alice was being torn between her marriage and our business, and since we always agreed that the correct order was God first, family second, and business third, she left the business to spend more time with her family.

I ran the business for several months by myself before help arrived. The Boddie and James families owned and operated a balloon business similar to ours in the Spanaway/Tacoma area. Forming a partnership with them gave us much-needed knowledge, experience, and help. The merging of our businesses was the answer to my prayers and theirs.

In time, we were commissioned to decorate events with our sculptures, arches, and other elegant balloon décor. We expanded to accommodate customer requests for floral displays and arrangements. One of our most memorable experiences was sculpting two huge fifty-foot-long, ten-foot-wide colorful Chinese dragons—each with its own rippling tail—to be hung from the ceiling of a casino on an ocean liner. We worked all night on that job. It was so rewarding to hear people respond with "oohs" and "aahs" at the sight of our elaborate creation.

We decorated weddings, expos, school proms, class reunions, and many major corporate events. Our slogans were "Ba'Loonnie Toone Lane, where there's a party every day!" and "If it's worth celebrating, it's worth decorating!"

CHAPTER SIX

DÉJÀ VU

"Wanting something is not enough. You must hunger for it.
Your motivation must be absolutely compelling in order to overcome
the obstacles that will invariably come your way."

All of my mother's grandchildren and great grandchildren call her Muggie. The name stemmed from her grandchildren's mispronunciation of the word *grandmother*, which sounded more like "granmugger." Over time, it was translated to Mugger and then to Muggie.

In 1988, Mother and Lovell separated and divorced. She moved from Hawaii, where Lovell had been stationed since 1983, and lived in Denver for a few months before settling in Washington State. There she enjoyed being close to her children and grandchildren.

It had been a long time since she had seen my brother Kevin, who was stationed in Germany. In 1995, Kevin and his family were about to complete their last overseas tour before retiring from the Army. Mother had missed other opportunities to visit Kevin and me in Germany, so she and her friend Mona decided to travel abroad to visit his family and tour Europe. The evening after their arrival, they were all sitting comfortably in the living room after dinner reminiscing about the adventures of our past. All of a sudden, Mother felt faint.

"Her eyes just rolled backwards, and she passed out," Kevin recalled.

My mother was rushed to the local German hospital. She had suffered, of all things, a brain aneurysm. She made it through the surgery but slipped into a coma and was paralyzed on the entire left side of her body.

Surie and I made arrangements to take a military flight to Germany. Alice housesat and took care of all the children. Kevin and his wife, Toni, were very busy making major medical decisions. Simultaneously, they were also trying to declare Mother as Kevin's dependent because she had no medical insurance. Mother was now totally financially and physically dependent upon Kevin's support. The benefit of being Kevin's dependent automatically entitled her to military medical coverage.

The aneurysm ruptured at the perfect time. The following day Mother would have been on a bus for a sightseeing tour. If she had been home, she probably would have been alone when she fainted. In either scenario, she might not have received medical treatment soon enough to save her life.

The day Surie and I arrived in Germany, we gave Mother a homemade audiotape of six of her grandchildren singing and talking to her. What I remember most about making the tape was Murice. He was four years old at the time and spoke into the tape recorder as if it were a telephone.

"Muggie, it's me, Murice. I love you. Muggie, can you hear me? Hey, where you at?" he yelled into the recorder as he waited for Mother's response.

That's exactly what she needed, someone yelling at her and calling her back to this world. Subconsciously, Mother received the very message she needed to hear. I've been told that comatose patients can hear what we say to them. So we set the tape recorder next to Mother's bed and played it very loudly, over and over again. This entertained her German roommates, who thought the small voices and songs sounded so cute.

The next afternoon, on the seventeenth day of Mother's coma, she opened her eyes. Later Mother told us that the tape was her first memory of consciousness and had helped her make the journey back.

Mother's friend Mona flew back to Washington on her scheduled return flight. Mother legally became Kevin's dependent and was transferred to a military hospital—in Landstuhl, Germany, of course. As Kevin, Surie, and I entered that familiar facility, it was like déjà vu. Though Dr. Klara was no longer stationed there, we walked down the same ward for the same medical condition that had stricken Surie ten years earlier. I felt like I was reliving an experience I would rather have not repeated.

Mother stayed in the hospital in Landstuhl for about one week before she was stable enough to be transported to Fort Lewis Medical Center in Washington State. Although the statistics are low for aneurysm survivors—approximately eight out of ten patients don't survive—my mother held on. She held on to the fact that her very own son-in-law had survived the same condition.

After several weeks at Fort Lewis, Mother slowly overcame the paralysis and no longer needed medical treatment. She was transferred to Good Samaritan Hospital near our home for physical therapy. She spent months recuperating and learning how to walk again. Alice would throw a pillow on the floor to see if Mother could bend down, pick it up, and stand up again on her own. At the time, Mother needed help with this task, but we wouldn't assist her—tough love was required. Mother expressed over and over again how much she wanted to leave the hospital. In her mind, she could take care of herself. She couldn't then, but eventually she was able to.

After recuperating, Mother moved in with Surie and me and continued her therapy as an outpatient. We eventually moved her to an apartment building for senior citizens. She also had an aide that came over daily to help her with her needs.

Mother was definitely on the road to recovery. She became spunkier than I had ever seen her before. Sometimes I didn't recognize her new personality, or boldness. After marrying at the age of sixteen, having eight children, dealing with two divorces, surviving a brain aneurysm, coma, and paralysis, she started college at the age of 69. Mother graduated with honors in June 2006. That September, at the age of 74, she began studies for her master's degree in applied behavioral science.

CHAPTER SEVEN

ALICE IN WONDERLAND

*"Fear does not have any special power
unless you empower it by submitting to it."*

When Surie and I returned from Germany, it was just in the nick of time. Alice was helping out at Ba'loonnie Toone Lane and sharing way too much information with a bride-to-be.

"Girl, I know you love him today, but ten years from now, it's just not gonna be the same," she said. I had to cut her off quickly before our client walked out the door. Weddings had become our bread and butter.

Unfortunately, even though Alice had left the business to spend more time with her family, eventually she and her husband of thirteen years separated. She moved in with my family to regroup and find comfort. My sister used this much-needed time for herself, reexamining her life. She took classes at Pierce College and got a job with a local high school as a security guard on campus. She won the affection of the students, who shared their lives with her. And, in time, they treated her more like a counselor/therapist than a security guard.

In a way, her stay at our home was a return of the Three Musketeers. Surie, Alice, and I were together again, with a few additional characters—all of our children. Her children spent weekends with us and weekdays with their father so as not to interrupt their school schedule. Alice felt that working for the school district was the perfect job. She knew this position would allow her the freedom to be off during the summer months to spend quality time with Lareina and Arsenio.

Working at her new job and living with us, Alice was able to save enough money for a deposit and monthly rent on a one-bedroom apartment. In January 1996, she moved into her own place, but with bittersweet emotions. While she was so excited about this new beginning, she was consumed with sadness over her family's separation.

∽

In May 1996, our brother David, who had a history of disturbing the peace, was released from jail. He was set free around 12:30 in the morning with a pocketful of money. David was released with no plans, identification, or medication. He called my mother to find out if he could come to her apartment. Mother lived almost an hour away from where David was released. He took a taxi to her place.

My mother lived in a one-bedroom senior residence complex, where the occupancy rule was strictly enforced. When Alice found out the next morning that David was at mother's apartment, she knew he couldn't stay there. She also knew he needed a place to live, so she invited him to stay with her. Not wanting to disturb the weekend arrangements with her children, Alice explained to David how limited and valuable her family time was with Lareina and Arsenio. Since she only had her children from Friday night through Sunday evening, she didn't want that time interrupted with explanations of Uncle David's unusual behavior. Alice told David that he was welcome to stay during the week, but over the weekends he would need to go to a nearby shelter.

Alice's kind heart wouldn't allow her to leave or put our brother out on the street. It's just that motherhood overruled family hospitality. So each Friday, the ritual began. My sister would return home from work with her usual list of local shelters. She agreed to drop him off and pick him up. Each week, David reluctantly packed his clothes for the stay at the less glorious accommodations, but by the third week, his reluctance turned into resentment. Alice sensed his unwillingness and decided to approach him two days earlier on a Wednesday, giving him ample time to procrastinate before the weekend began rather than over the weekend.

I called her at the apartment that evening. "She was here, but now she's gone," David told me. Alice hadn't mentioned she was going anywhere after work, so I expected her to be at home. But David couldn't tell me anything about her whereabouts and quickly changed the subject. He wanted to tell me what a good time he had had at the family gathering I hosted at my home ten days prior. He said that he appreciated me putting it all together.

The gathering was held for Lovell, who was in town from Hawaii. We welcomed his visit with a big Sunday afternoon soul food dinner, which everyone enjoyed. What I like about our family is that even in-laws are never outlaws. Since David had been in jail, this gathering was like a mini family reunion for him as well.

I appeased David and listened, noticing an unusual calmness in his voice. Even back in the day, David's voice was always full of excitement and urgency as he tried to get his point across. Finding Alice was the main thing on my mind, so I dismissed my straying thoughts and ended the conversation.

"I had a good time too. Tell Alice to call me when she comes home. Talk to you later."

I made a series of additional phone calls but didn't reach Alice. A half hour later, I phoned her apartment again. This time there was only ring after ring, then her answering machine. My thoughts wandered back to the phone conversation with David. An eerie feeling raced through me that grew stronger with every passing thought. I didn't know what, but something was definitely wrong. Around 9:30 p.m., I asked Surie to drive to Alice's apartment to see if her car was in the parking lot. I stayed home by the phone in the hope that one of the many calls I placed earlier would be returned.

"Alice's car isn't here," Surie told me from his cell phone.

With Alice's apartment on the ground level, Surie could see there were no lights on inside. When he returned home, we both tried to sleep but couldn't. The evening turned to late night, and still no Alice. About four in the morning, the ringing of our telephone startled me.

"David just called," Mother said. He returned home and found that someone had broken into Alice's apartment! He said Alice was hurt! I told him to hang up and call 911."

I threw on some clothes and hurried to pick up my mother. I didn't want to go to Alice's apartment but to the hospital if that's where she had been taken, but first I needed to find out which hospital. Mother and I returned to my home and I called Alice's apartment again. There was no answer. I called the police station to find out if they were actually at her place and what hospital she had been transported to. The dispatch officer informed me the police officers were there, but she couldn't give me any additional information.

For background noise, I turned on the television set. The five o'clock morning news was on. Suddenly the drum roll sound that indicates breaking news caught everyone's attention. The screen abruptly turned to a solid blue inset with bold red letters that read "Special Report." Our eyes fixed on the TV, we heard the announcer briefly state: "African-American woman found deceased early this morning in her Lakewood apartment."

My body turned cold as ice. I could almost feel my blood drain from the top of my head to the sole of my soul in an instant. The announcer might as well have pronounced Alice's full name and social security number. With every fiber of my being, I knew the broadcaster was talking about my sister.

First I called Alice's husband to inform him of the alleged break-in at Alice's apartment and the special report I had just heard. Determined to get concrete answers, I again called the Lakewood Police Department for more information. I gave the officer my sister's name and address and asked what was going on at her apartment. I got the same response, with the exception of one clue that answered everything. The police officer said she couldn't give out anymore information . . . about the scene.

"The scene! What do you mean the scene?" I demanded to know. She didn't say anything, but now I knew everything.

Surie dressed Angela and Murice, and we took them to my sister Susan's house. We didn't tell our children much and wanted to leave them in the familiar comfort of my sister's home. Then Surie, Mother, and I headed to Alice's apartment. I drove cautiously, my mind racing with questions, pondering this nightmare. Not until a quarter of a mile or so past Alice's cross street did any of us notice I had missed the turn. Maybe all of us wanted to avoid what we subconsciously knew— something terrible had happened to our Alice.

I got back on track and headed down her block. Once I turned the corner, there were flashing red and blue police lights that guided us directly to Alice's front door. As we drove closer, the scene became more horrifying: a fleet of police vehicles in the parking lot, yellow tape blocking the entrance and surrounding area to my sister's apartment building, reporters scrambling to get more information on the news.

When we arrived at Alice's apartment around six o'clock in the morning, a police officer quickly came over to find out who we were and sadly confirmed our worst fears. The newscasters had gotten the main fact right, as much as I wished they hadn't. The African-American woman in the special report was indeed my sister, Alice.

Every single cell and nerve in my body from head to toe was traumatized, but not even that feeling could surpass the devastation in my heart. I went into shock and cried out of control. I grew numb; my brain wouldn't even allow me to think straight. The police officer spoke, but all I could see were his lips moving. I couldn't make sense of the words he was saying or even hear the sobs of my family.

After about an hour, I regained strength and was stable

enough to go with Surie, Mother, and Susan's husband, Steve, to the police station for questioning. While waiting, I had time to go outside to the pay phone to call my father. I needed to speak with him. His line was busy, which was unusual, just as the day had been. I hung up, feeling more alone than ever before. I was trying to hear the voice of my father, but when I attempted to call him again, another voice spoke out from behind me.

"Hey!" the voice whispered.

The instant I heard it, I turned around. It was Alice's voice. I could recognize that soft-pitched, cheerful sound that was uniquely my sister's tone anywhere. I wanted to see Alice badly so I could quickly write this event off as a nightmare. But there was no Alice, only the clear, cool spring May morning, a glorious day for most. She wasn't there; I saw no one. But I didn't give up easily. I looked around the corner, hoping to see my sister there alive and well.

I cried as I called out her name, then became very still and listened intensely for her voice again. Some might say it was a figment of my imagination, or maybe I was just hallucinating. I believe God will meet you where you are and speak to you in a familiar voice that's comforting to you. After several silent minutes passed, shrill reality hit me again. I refocused and called my father once more. This time he answered. He had already seen the morning news and knew his "baby," the one he affectionately called Alley, was gone.

No one will ever truly know what transpired at Alice's apartment. No other families were home in the four-unit complex that evening to hear her cries. When Surie went to Alice's apartment that evening, her car wasn't there because David had taken it. For years, Surie continued to beat himself up about this. He felt he should have banged on the door, even though no lights were on.

"She could've still been alive at that time," he insisted.

"It's a lose-lose situation playing the 'what if' game," I told Surie. "It wasn't your fault. You shouldn't keep blaming yourself," I said, hoping to free him of his guilt.

Based on information provided by my mother, the police alleged that after Alice returned home from work as normal on Wednesday evening, she told David about an apartment he could rent on a cash-only basis. He became upset. A fight followed, ending in my sister's death.

David did his best to deny the crime at first. He fabricated a portrayal that blamed Alice's death on an intruder. When that scenario didn't work, he changed his story and accused her husband. My family and I knew that wasn't true. Alice's husband would never do something like this. But David's unpredictability and his drug habit, we knew, were to blame instead.

The police recounted the scene for us and explained that Alice fought for her life. The scratches on David's hands and body made him their only suspect. Still, David had an excuse for everything, claiming the scratches came from a fight he had had earlier that same evening. It was discovered that this so-called fight was also fictitious.

All day long, the local television news ran stories of Alice's death. Thankfully, I was too busy to watch. Ba'Loonnie Toone Lane was scheduled to decorate an event at a hotel that afternoon. Though physically present, my mind was elsewhere, reminiscing about special times with Alice. My body went on autopilot. Even if you paid me, I still would not be able to recall the occasion, theme, or color scheme of that event. My mind blocked it out. I do remember that when the managers of the hotel heard what had happened, they couldn't believe we were there. They too cared for Alice and couldn't keep from crying. I could hear my father say, "Take care of business first, and cry later," and, boy, did I.

∽

Putting my grief aside wasn't easy and didn't happen for a long time. I thought I had reached the depth of heartache after my two miscarriages, but the pain of my sister's death was at a depth that I didn't even know existed. I became physically sick to my stomach. The day Surie told me he was married, I felt my heart crack, but this time it completely broke into a million little pieces, and it literally ached. I couldn't eat or sleep. I was completely emotionally shattered.

Initially, I didn't want anything to do with David. I couldn't even muster up the energy to hate him. Daily, I called Alice's answering machine, mainly to hear her voice at the end of the message say " . . . and have a perfect day." Nightly, my dreams were long and dreadful. Images of my sister at the time of her death filled my head. Even then, Alice and I were a team, both of us in her apartment fighting David together. I always awoke out of breath, startled, and sweating just before the fight would end. Every time I thought about her final minutes of struggle, I shut the images down, blocking them out, because I was simply unable to handle the truth. I still don't know the gruesome details and never intend to find out. I chose not to see the pictures of the scene, nor did I go to the morgue to see my sister's body. That's a memory I couldn't handle and didn't need.

When making balloon deliveries, I often found myself driving aimlessly, ending up on the other side of town, not knowing how I got there or how to return to the shop. Call it empathy or sympathy, I vicariously felt the weight of Alice's pain and felt the closeness we shared abruptly wrenched from me. Between her memorial service and the business, I didn't have the luxury of being homebound. Had I been, I believe I might have stayed in that stage of grief for months to years. At the time, a freight train could have hit me and the pain would not have compared to what I was going through inside. I couldn't even say the words "Alice is dead" out loud.

Still, a memorial service had to be planned. I decided I did not want to wake up one day and regret that I had not participated. This was not a dress rehearsal and there were no second chances or, for me, choices. Alice and I had been partners my entire life. And now that her earthly journey was complete, I would do for my sister what I know she would have done for me. Our children, ages five through seven at the time, were going to be at the service, and I didn't want this to be a frightening experience or a bad memory for any of them. We all agreed that her memorial would not be a funeral but rather a celebration of her life, and we decided against a casket. Alice's body was cremated.

I wanted the service to be uplifting, just as my sister was. I wanted her friends to know the Alice that I knew. I wanted people to walk away with a desire to do something useful with their lives, even if it was to be a professional clown. To ensure this outcome, I couldn't just delegate this task. This was extremely personal to me, and there was no time to waste. The perfectionist in me majored on the minors as I tended to every detail of the service. That "Be a now person" my mother always emphasized was being tested more than ever.

Planning Alice's service helped distract me from the reality of my grief. Through a river of tears, I wrote my list of things I needed to do and crossed off accomplishments, emotion by emotion.

Without realizing it, we had scheduled Alice's service for

the same afternoon as the graduating seniors' ceremony at the school where she had worked. There were so many seniors at her service, we wondered if their graduation ceremony had been rescheduled. That's how dear she was to them. I remember Alice's service from having planned the details. I was there physically, but mentally I wasn't. People said that the service was personal, uplifting, and beautiful, and that's exactly the memory of Alice I wanted her friends and family to be left with. Ironically, the last time I saw Alice was on Memorial Day 1996, a day of remembrance.

Video pictures helped recap Alice's life as the Mariah Carey song "Always Be My Baby" played softly in the background. Acting as her manager to the end, I arranged for my sister to sing at her own memorial service: one segment of the video featured Alice and me singing The Jackson Five's "Never Can Say Good-Bye." I knew she would have loved it and trusted her spirit looked on with delight.

My sister-in-law Clara sang "Blessed Assurance," and I invited a popular local singer, Korla Wygal, to sing "Separate Ways," a beautiful piece she had originally written after her mother passed.

Our florist, Loretta, from Ba'Loonnie Toone Lane, arranged beautiful floral bouquets, along with boutonnieres and corsages. Friends from Alice's previous jobs recited resolutions. The one from Ba'Loonnie Toone Lane read:

A RESOLUTION

Presented by: Ba'Loonnie Toone Lane

CELEBRATING THE LIFE WORK
OF ALICE MARGARET

WHEREAS from the very beginning it was about dreams, it was about hope, it was about family, it was about creating a legacy for her children, and

WHEREAS in November 1990, Alice and her sister Angela acted on their desires to be entrepreneurs by opening a balloon shop in Tacoma's Freighthouse Square, which Alice named Ba'Loonnie Toone Lane, and

WHEREAS fate would have it, the same week of their grand opening, Angela, who is a reservist in the United States Air Force, was activated into the Desert Storm War, leaving Alice alone to manage a brand new business for six months, and

WHEREAS Alice worked as a sales clerk, order clerk, bookkeeper, marketing manager, customer service specialist, business manager, and balloon artist—whatever it took to keep the business running and profitable in Angela's absence—and

WHEREAS it was Alice's vision that guided the two sisters to expand the business into an all-occasion floral and gift shop, and

WHEREAS it was Alice's vision, tenacity, and hard work that initiated a merger between Ba'Loonnie Toone Lane and another similar business called Span Tac: The Balloon Doctors, owned by Patricia James, Deidre Holmes, and Dorothy Boddie, and

WHEREAS these African-American women, who were competing in the same business market, understood and agreed that working together was the avenue to prosperity for them all, and

WHEREAS Alice took a time-out from Ba'Loonnie Toone Lane to advance her education and improve her skills, and

WHEREAS the most important thing in Alice's life was loving her children with all her heart and soul, and

WHEREAS Alice was taken from her children, family, and those who loved her dearly through a senseless act of violence, and

WHEREAS Alice will be remembered as a STRONG Black woman, who, even through the face of adversity and turmoil in her life, held her head high, kept her sense of humor, and gave of herself to help the lives of others,

NOW, BE IT THEREFORE RESOLVED that for the cause of stopping the violence, in memory of

ALICE MARGARET,

Let love begin at home.

After the service, we released a bouquet of brightly colored yellow, red, orange, green, blue, and purple balloons into the air. Then everyone headed to a local club Alice used to frequent. We closed the place down with Alice's friends singing karaoke songs of encouragement and comfort to my family. Sure enough, I wasn't ready for my sister to be a memory, but this wasn't about me. This was how Alice would have planned to end her life's story—with a blast, a celebration, a party. And so it was.

Everything went as planned, ending the most emotionally challenging week of my entire life. Even though I didn't gain a sense of finality when the service was completed, I felt a sense of peace and knew this was the first step on my road to recovery. After Alice's service, for the first time in a week I was able to eat and smile. But I still couldn't say the words "Alice is dead" out loud. I was pleased and relieved that her service was behind us and that now my family could move forward with the process of healing and forgiving.

To honor Alice's life, my sister Sharon and I formed an awareness group called Love Begins at Home, which focused on violence within the family. Our meetings were more like counseling sessions for me. At the same time we were discussing the effects of violence within the family, we were learning lessons from Alice's death. We looked to our past to pinpoint where the violence began. My father admitted he had treated the boys much more harshly than the girls. Though we each had the same set of rules, the consequences differed greatly and, unfortunately, people who are hurt, hurt other people. My father thinks his stern disciplinary actions may have contributed to David's aggressive behavior, but, thankfully, he stops short of blaming himself for the outcome.

Needless to say, the balloon business wasn't the joy it used to be. Day by day it became a full-time job just to focus on what now became work. Sharon gave me a tape with Patti LaBelle singing a song called "Love Never Dies." I played that song every single day. The words soothed my aching heart when no one else could help me. They helped me to realize that your spirit just transforms from form to formless. That song, along with about five others related to death, were included in my grief-relief tape. I played my "music therapy" tape so often that I have had to re-record it several times over the years.

∽

My brother's trial began a year after Alice's death. It was very hard for us to relive the details. Some family members were summoned to testify for the defense, others for the prosecution. We didn't allow this to divide us; the situation was already bad enough. None of us mumbled one negative word toward my mother for standing up for her son.

I was subpoenaed by the prosecution regarding the phone conversation I had with David the evening of Alice's death. Because I was called as a witness, I was not allowed to hear anyone else's testimony before me. During the two-week trial, I spent day after day secluded, on standby in the hallway. Daily, the lawyers prepared me to take the stand. However, as it turned out, my testimony wasn't needed. I was so grateful. It was still too painful to discuss Alice's death, let alone to be aggressively questioned about it. I was only allowed to be before the jurors during the closing arguments, which was more than enough for me.

When I finally entered the courtroom, I saw the enlarged pictures of the crime scene. With everything in me, I did my best to ignore the images, but my mind still visualized them. Thankfully, the photos were positioned at an angle for only the jurors to view.

Slow, deep breaths helped me endure the lawyers' final statements defending and prosecuting my siblings. Not far from us sat my brother David. I can't tell you what his demeanor was because I didn't look at him. I didn't know what feelings to expect, and I couldn't bring myself to look in his eyes for fear of the emotions that would arise from within me.

CHAPTER EIGHT

FORGIVENESS

*"If you are carrying strong feelings about something
that happened in your past, they may hinder
your ability to live in the present."*

My family knew of two things for sure: David's mental frailty and his love for Alice. Knowing this, we were able to separate the man from his behavior. Deep down, we knew David didn't have a killer's heart, and we never desired him to be in a facility that treated him as such. He needed to be in a mental hospital, not a penitentiary.

Once David's delusions ceased and he realized what he had done, he took full responsibility and profusely apologized to anyone who would listen. He was so extremely remorseful for Alice's death that he had to be placed in a padded cell to protect him from himself. Many people fail to realize that David also suffered the loss of his sister, whom he loved very deeply. If he had been released from jail with his medication, this would have allowed him to live in his right mind, and he would never have hurt Alice. In fact, it would have been just the opposite. He sincerely repented and would have given anything and everything for things to have been different that evening. His letters detail his remorse:

April 21, 1999

Dear Angela, Surie, & Family,

I hope this letter reaches you in the best of joy and health. I am glad to have this opportunity to write to you and ask for your forgiveness. Please forgive me for what I have done. It was by no means intentional or deliberate.

During the time of this awful incident, I suffered extremely with schizophrenia and bipolar disorder, the symptoms of which I have suffered and lived with most of my life.

The prosecuting attorney in this case said that it was all because of the use of drugs ... not so. But I admit that drugs did not help my condition any, nor have they helped. Though at times I have used drugs to ease the pain and confusion, they only left me in a worse situation.

This is a very hard lesson for me to depend on God for health and a sound mind, and I am truly sorry that Alice was put through this. I am also very sorry that everyone else was put through this, especially Lareina and Arsenio.

I pray that Alice's children grow with love, understanding, and forgiveness instead of the negative side of this and that God blesses their lives with peace and happiness and a positive outlook on life in spite of this unfortunate occurrence. I pray this blessing for everyone. If you could understand, just a little, my disposition in this situation, you would also understand my gratitude for your forgiveness. No, this is not an easy thing to deal with, but I believe that God has forgiven me also.

Love,
David

∽

September 29, 2001

Uncle Billy,

How are you and everyone there? Blessed I'm sure. I, myself, am maintaining, growing spiritually and am blessed as well, even here, even now. God's love is not only healing my heart and mind, but His truth does set my soul free. I don't know if I'll ever get out of here physically; however, the freedom and love I now treasure is within.

I've learned to be forgiving, as God has bestowed the promise of His great forgiveness upon me. Early on, when I came to prison, I was very heavy with sorrow and filled with shame. Nothing made sense at all except reaching out to our great and loving Father, which was all I could do and, by grace, all I needed to do.

Then one day, through the tears and the pain, as I sat in my cell searching my tired and heavy ladened soul, I searched the scripture, I heard Him speaking to me. Never before had I felt love this way, as this (sweet) sense of love imparted His message through this scripture: "'Come now, and let us reason together,' says the Lord. 'Though your sins are like scarlet, they shall be as white as snow.'" (Isaiah 1:18) And through the reason of His great mercy, I knew with my deepest heart that God had forgiven me for the death of Alice.

I tell you, my soul has not been the same since; the heaviness, the pain, and the shame were truly lifted. And even though it seems to reappear, it does so only as clouds that melt away before the radiance of His magnificent light. I have a guitar here with me, which is a real blessing. Often I sit here in my cell alone with Christ playing, singing, and writing songs of His love. My soul becomes very peaceful amid the backdrop of an atmosphere that can be chaotic and stressful. To express and refresh my heart with praise and songs of His love does lift me above it all.

I used to sing and play in the chapel here on Sundays for a few years. It was an honor and a blessing. But things have changed and I no longer sing in the chapel here on Sundays. But I will be transferring soon and look forward to singing in the chapel there.

Love,
David

Having David as an adversary wasn't necessary. Who would that benefit? Not to forgive my brother would block any blessings that God had in store for me. Hatred is so heavy, taxing, and a waste of time and energy. Besides, as they say, WWJD (What would Jesus do)? Over time, David's remorsefulness caused even my distance to dissipate. Some pain you won't forget, but through forgiveness, understanding, and love, you can remember the events from a different perspective. David's nightly nightmares, deeply embedded in his mind, were living hell enough. I wouldn't wish that punishment on anyone. My nonforgiveness could not have brought him any lower, yet my forgiveness made a world of difference in both of our states of mind.

Alice was such a giving and forgiving person that harboring unforgiveness toward David would not have honored her life. The fact is, Alice was our family's favorite. Throughout her life, she intuitively connected with each one of us on our own individual level. At our children's birthday parties, she always added an extra seat during musical chairs because she wanted everyone to be a winner. On Mother's Day 1996, she gifted beautiful plants of appreciation to friends and family who had given time and attention to Lareina and Arsenio after her separation from her husband.

Alice's life was taken so suddenly that it left me without closure. I needed something to seal the gap between her life and death. I longed for answers; I sought and prayed for them daily. Even though Alice once told me that someone had prophesied she would pass before she turned forty, this didn't give me the peace I needed.

My comfort came after the trial was complete from none other than Alice herself. When the police released to us Alice's belongings that had been held in evidence, I found my peace buried in her purse inside her wallet. Hidden deep within the folds, where you would store your last dollar bill saved "for emergency use only," there was a letter she had written to God. Neither the police nor the lawyers had discovered this letter.

Alice's letter was better than any amount of money she might have willed. After I read the first sentence, I felt the grief I had carried for the last year instantly vanish. I finally received the peace I had been praying for. Alice's letter opened with:

Dear God,

Hello. It's me, Alice. I need you. I can't handle my affairs without you.

She could have stopped right there. That was all I needed. She was talking directly to God, surrendering and accepting His will. Who am I to question our Lord and Saviour? She asked God to handle her affairs, and He allowed her to come home. As close as I was to Alice, I was not experiencing the extent of her suffering. I wasn't going through a divorce, my family

DEAR GOD

HELLO

It's ME ALICE I NEED you I CAN'T hANDLE My AFFAIRS without you. I NEED to GiVE My MOTHER heR CAR BACK AND GeT ONE OF my OWN. Build up the LOVE & RESPECT that My ChildREN hAVE FOR ME. REMOVE my BROTHER FROM My APARTMENT. Build up MONEY iN My SAVINGS ACCOUNT. BUY SOME Clothes(A NEW RWARDROBE). PUT SOME FURNITURE & PlANTS iN My APARTMENT. AND Build UP My SELF EsTEEM & LOVE FOR mySELF. Also GET My Body iN STRONG FIRM physiCAL ShApE.

GOD PlEASE GiVE ME the STRENth & the pATiENCE TO PUT My LiFE BACK IN ORDER AGAiN. THANK-you LOVE AliCE wasn't separated, and I couldn't feel her pain or cry her tears. The moment she died, she was no longer hurting.

There was no date on the letter, but from the content, I could tell it was written within two weeks of her passing because she wrote about David being in her apartment. I read the letter over and over, searching for the message, the blessing, and the miracle. Though the letter was addressed "Dear God," not "Dear Angela," it was for me. I felt her passing so personally that I had been crying out, "Why did you leave me?" But then I realized that her death wasn't about me. For that matter, her death was not about David either. As I witnessed Alice's surrender to God, I was finally able to do the same. With each reading of her letter, I became healthier in accepting her death, stronger in my faith, and forgiving in my heart.

God knew I needed this message from Alice for my healing process and that this was the perfect time for me to receive it. He knows our needs before we are formed in our mother's womb, just as the scripture says: "For your Father knows the things you have need of before you ask Him." (Matthew 6:8)

My mother was the first to forgive David. The rest of us were only able to forgive when the burden became too heavy to bear. Ultimately we learned that forgiveness truly is a gift that you give to yourself.

My father made the biggest improvement. I prayed that he would stop considering David as dead. God answers prayers.

Seven years later, he went to visit David for the first time. Several people were at that particular visit. Though there wasn't much spoken between David and my father, my father's presence alone spoke volumes. I believe that the visit was more beneficial for my father than it was for David and that his forgiveness probably saved his life. The hatred and bitterness he had felt toward his son was affecting his health, killing him slowly. His season of grief was headed directly toward a self-inflicted death sentence. His willingness to forgive was God softening his heart. What a major miracle! Like my father, we don't always make the right decision at first, but there comes a time when we can make the decision right.

David has many talents. He's an excellent writer, communicator, and musician. He taught himself how to play the guitar, and he sings very well. He now uses those gifts to praise God for His mercy. The judge gave him life, but God sentenced him to success. My mother now conducts forgiveness workshops. "Unforgiveness is a matter of misunderstanding," she teaches.

I have realized in life that sometimes what appears to be the end is really a new beginning. I moved from the pain of saying "Alice is dead" out loud to realizing that the day of Alice's death was only one day out of the thirty-nine years and seven months of her remarkable life. That day was not a monument, but a moment of her earthly journey. I then knew that Ba'Loonnie

Toone Lane was so much more than just decorating parties and weddings. God allowed Alice and me our desired daily dose of togetherness, filled with invaluable fun times and memories. Our partnership was a continuation of our childhood. Now that I had my mind in the proper perspective, I was able to honor a lifetime of wonderful memories with Alice, my funny friend, ace, smart business partner, my sister sista. I was finally able to say the words "Alice is dead" out loud.

CHAPTER NINE

MOVING FORWARD

*"The only limits to the possibilities in your life tomorrow
are the 'buts' you use today."*

Each day, Tacoma became smaller. The balloon business kept me quite busy but was no longer rewarding. I visualized my sister in her usual place to my left each time I decorated an event. She wasn't there, nor would she ever be again. So after seven years of owning and operating Ba'Loonnie Toone Lane, I turned over my stake in the business to my partners.

I began to literally crave more sunshine in my life, certainly more than the rainy state of Washington could provide. My daughter, Angela, had a lot to do with us considering sunny Southern California. From a very young age, she had always dreamed of becoming a famous actress. As early as three, she shared her claim to fame with everyone who would listen: "I'm a star. The world just doesn't know it yet!" she often said.

So devoted was Angela to her goal that acting classes and monologues consumed more of her time than treasured childhood milestones like learning to jump double-Dutch or riding a bike. At seven, she still couldn't cycle, so Murice, though two years younger, teasingly rode circles around her. Embarrassed over her ineptness, Angela asked that cycling lessons occur only during the evening so no one would see her fall. Despite our efforts, cycling eluded her for the time being, and she gave up.

"Angela, you need to learn to ride a bike in case you're given a script that requires riding a bicycle," I insisted, attempting to come from a place I knew she was passionate about.

"Mother! That's what stunt doubles are for," she reminded me. On that note, I packaged her bike, adorned it with a bow and gave it to her cousin Lareina.

To make sure our decision to move was a sound one and not just an emotional whim, Surie and I waited a year after Alice's death to see if we still felt the same about relocating. Such an important decision warranted sufficient prayer and planning. In time, we knew California was the ideal place, not only for our budding actress, who did earn a spot in an International Modeling and Talent Association competition held in Los Angeles, but also for my family to begin anew.

In October 1997, I went to Southern California to look at homes. When I arrived, Marlene and Kathryn, my realtors, picked me up from the airport and took me to my Aunt Fedora's home nearby. That night, my cousin Juanita suggested I also consider some homes she knew about. The next day, the realtors and I made these suggested homes our first stop. Extremely extravagant, the houses resembled soap opera homes, the type that should remain untouched by children. As elegant as they were, I couldn't see paying such a high mortgage when many of the rooms were already too small for my growing children.

We got back on track and drove to the homes on the realtors' list. The prices of these homes were just right and had everything I had told them I was looking for. Even the school district was top notch. However, when the realtors parked and got out of the car, I didn't move. Everything within told me my home wasn't in this area. The feeling was too strong to ignore, so I didn't bother taking off my seatbelt.

I told the realtors my home wasn't in this neighborhood. "What do you mean? This area has everything on your list," Kathryn said.

I knew she was right, but at the same time, I just wasn't moved to move, so I didn't. When the Holy Spirit speaks, I have learned to listen.

"Well, if this isn't the area for your home, then where is it?" one of the women asked condescendingly.

I sensed but ignored the sarcasm and focused instead on my inner thoughts. I didn't know the area, so I sat quietly, gazed out the window, and passed the question over to God.

"If this isn't the location for my home, then where is it?" I repeated under my breath. Ordinarily, Alice and my husband would have been my "consultants." Neither one was here, so God had become my sole source and chief advisor.

"It's not in this area, but it's close to the homes my cousin mentioned," I finally said.

My realtor and her trainee looked at each other as if I was crazy. Their car doubled as an office, equipped with a laptop, maps, telephone, etc. "Let's look at the map together, and then show me what's east and west of the area we've just come from," I asserted.

Really, it was the Holy Spirit prompting me. They noted there were several tract homes in that area that were not yet completed, but one tract had three models ready for viewing. I asked Marlene to call and see if they were open. They were.

I was very nervous on the drive back across town. What if I didn't like the new tract homes? Would I ask the realtors to return to the location we had just left? Even now, it's hard for me to believe I never looked at the homes the realtors had preselected for me.

The first model was nice but, again, too small for my growing family and huge German furniture. But when we reached the second house, I knew I had found what I was looking for. It was big, beautiful, and equipped with everything on my list! Then we looked upstairs.

"This house is perfect, but in my dream home the laundry

room is upstairs," I jokingly noted. I didn't have that on my list, but the Holy Spirit knew the secret petitions of my heart.

"Oh, that floor plan is next door," said the realtor showing the homes.

I couldn't get out of that house fast enough and made a beeline for Model Home Three. As soon as I opened the door, I knew it was the prototype of my future home. It was so inviting, warm, and spacious. The Lord wanted me to have everything on my list and then some. The mountain view out of the north windows was magnificent, the floor plan was beautiful, and the school district was excellent. Even against pressure and logic, listening to that still, small voice of the Holy Spirit guided me to my family's brand new home.

I didn't hesitate one moment. That very day, I signed on the dotted line and paid the deposit. Stunned, my realtors had never experienced anything like this before and couldn't believe I was getting such a great deal.

"This house has more to offer than anything we planned to show you," they confessed. I kind of figured that was the case, but hearing it was confirmation. God is sooooo good!

∽

We moved to California in January 1998. The hardest thing about departing Washington was leaving Lareina and Arsenio. At the time, all I could do was assure them that my home was their home and they could come and visit every summer and during school breaks.

We videotaped the construction of our new house, room by room, and slept on air mattresses in a two-bedroom apartment, eagerly waiting to move into our home. The excitement of a new home and new school didn't stop Angela and Murice from missing their cousins and friends in Washington. Despite the move, Angela achieved Student of the Month fairly quickly, and Murice easily transferred the love he had for his second grade teacher in Washington to his new teacher in California.

Our furniture arrived April 1, 1998, and we moved in on schedule to become one of the first families in the subdivision. Soon after, our neighborhood began filling nicely with God-loving and friendly people. Life was good.

Fortunately, Surie and I were able to give our children a lot of quality time. Since neither of us worked full time, we devoted our energy to our family. We volunteered in our children's everyday activities wherever and whenever needed. On Sundays, we helped out in Sunday school to make sure our children learned the most important lesson of all—God's love for them. Each week, they looked forward to attending Abundantland, the children's ministry at Abundant Living Family Church, and they always invited their neighborhood friends to join us. I believe our hands-on approach to parenting has been the key ingredient to making our family work.

Being so blessed with Surie's renewed health compelled us to look for ways to be a blessing. We decided to become foster parents through a foster agency called Childhelp USA. After applying and meeting all the qualifications, we had a family meeting and decided to open our home and hearts to one boy around seven years old, Murice's age. Despite our preference, the foster care agency asked if we would consider a nine-year-old girl named Angelina.

"Angelina! Does she have a nickname?" said Surie. "Can we call her Lucy instead? You mean I now have two Angelas and an Angelina? I'm going to need a special speech therapy session just to keep the names straight!" he joked.

With a name like that, of course, I couldn't resist. We welcomed Angelina into our home and family. Tall and thin, Angelina had been in the foster care system since she was three years old. She was the oldest of four siblings, who were also separated from their parents and from one another. At first, Angelina quietly observed her new environment. Unfortunately, she had been in abusive foster homes in the past, so she took her time checking us out. With each passing day, she realized she was safe and began slowly letting us into her heart as she became a part of ours.

Angelina was the younger sister that Angela never had or asked for. Like typical siblings, they had their days, but outside the house they dared anyone to mess with the other. They got along better than I had expected, considering Angela never wanted to share her room with anyone. As much as we enjoyed Angelina, she didn't qualify as a brother for Murice.

"Angelina, she's okay, but she's a girl," Murice would say. "Where's my brother?" he'd whisper in my ear several times a day to remind me of our family's original decision.

For many months, Murice made sure our social worker knew he was still waiting for his brother. Surie and I didn't need to discuss it any further. We were happy and content with our family of three children. In spite of our decision, several months after Angelina joined our family the social worker tried to talk to us about boys who needed a home as well. One day, the social worker came by and again gave us that pleading look. I returned it with a don't-go-there stare.

"No, and please don't mention the child's name this time," I thought to myself. Naming the children made it seem as if we were rejecting them individually in a personal way rather than simply rejecting the agency's request.

However, before the words were out of my mouth, she said "Roger!"

The sound of his name resonated in our hearts, and at that very moment Surie and I looked at one another.

"Here we grow again!" we said in unison.

It's not like she hadn't mentioned the names of other boys, but this one touched our spirit. It was God opening and softening our hearts, letting us know this was the boy for our family. We couldn't get to Roger fast enough. We wanted to know all about him: What did he have for dinner that evening?

Was he tucked in bed nice and warm? How was he doing in school? We bombarded the social worker with all kinds of questions. Most of all, we wanted Roger to know he was a member of our family and he was wanted in our home.

Such good news made Murice do something I had never seen before—clean his room without being told. He excitedly prepared for his brother's arrival by dividing his space in half.

The instant we met Roger, all of our feelings were confirmed. Murice and Roger shared a genuine camaraderie that gained strength with each conversation and playful exchange. Murice was in the second grade, and Roger was in the first. They bonded immediately like long-lost brothers. This new relationship meant Murice now had a friend-in-residence, someone to play with and grow with. Roger made all the difference. In Roger, Murice had a companion of his own who accepted and embraced him without pretense.

It had been customary for the boys on the block to tease Murice about his short frame of three feet seven inches, especially during basketball games. Yet, in spite of his height, Murice knew he had major skills, like guarding and passing, that were impressive. But the kids only valued the most recognizable attribute of basketball players—height—and ridiculed anyone who lacked it.

Often Murice would return home from play with tears in his eyes. While Surie always applied the same hackneyed adage,

"Boys will be boys," to these situations, the protective mother in me wanted to go out and fight his battles. I made a point of speaking with the children and their parents. Still, nothing was resolved until Murice acquired a bigger brother. Roger qualified for big brother status despite being seven months younger than Murice. His presence alone was enough to defend against the neighborhood teasers. With Roger as his new sidekick, Murice's social status on the block improved remarkably.

Murice and Roger were so close that sometimes their relationship scared me. After just a few months, I couldn't imagine the boys ever being separated. It was certainly a possibility. As a foster child, Roger's biological parents still had parental rights and could reenter his life if they regained the privilege.

In the midst of caring for four children and all of the activity that this brought to our household, I soon found little time to worry about the chance that Roger and Angelina might leave. The new school year, of course, was a bit more stressful than summertime. Between four children, there were always book reports, spelling tests, or science projects due. Angelina required extra attention, so I was up late many nights tutoring, building skills, and, more importantly, bolstering her self-esteem. Nevertheless, I enjoyed being able to say I had a second, third, fourth, and fifth grader. Watching their bodies extend and their minds expand was my labor of love, guided by God's hands.

Our summers, which included Lareina and Arsenio, were

filled with family camping, Fourth of July block parties, adventure parks, traveling, and more. Between Surie and me, there were also annual family reunions. With our new family of six, and sometimes eight, flying wasn't in the budget, so we drove. From the West Coast to the East and back again, we stopped for visits with family and friends along the way.

Roger, who had become the family comedian, especially on the road trips, kept us laughing all the way. He introduced our family to a game he called "Make Me Laugh." Despite the title, the purpose of the game was for the audience members not to laugh or even crack a smile while the performing "comedian" did everything he could to make us do just the opposite. Each time, I came prepared with my game face on, but in no time at all Roger would have us in stitches with all of his impersonations, voices, and sound effects. He was a natural stand-up comedian—he had lots of jokes, his timing was right on, and his material was spontaneous and hilarious. The first person to laugh was out of the game. Murice was his biggest fan and always the first one to smile or burst into a contagious giggle from Roger's comical talents. The whole family would usually join in with a hearty, belly-aching laugh.

Everyone could see that Murice and Roger genuinely enjoyed each other's company. Their strong bond reminded me of my relationship with Alice. I couldn't have been happier knowing my son shared the same type of closeness I once had with my sister.

∽

I sat in church on Sunday morning, January 8, 2000, second service, second row, and Pastor Diego Mesa asked the congregation, "Does your family know what Jesus has done for you lately?"

I didn't know why at the time, but I was moved with great urgency to write letters to seven members of my family and answer this very question. The question affected me so intensely that I began to reflect on my life. I was embarrassed as I wrote my thoughts on the back of the church program, but by the time the service ended, I had completed the outline of my letter to my family.

Within two days, I wrote the letter and mailed it. I didn't get much reaction from my family members about my correspondence. However, it wasn't about my family; it was about my relationship with God. It was my confirmation that my personal struggle with death had ended. My road to recovery was complete, and I was spiritually and physically healed. Here is the letter I wrote:

January 10, 2000

Dear Family,

While sitting in church, the question of the day was "Does your family know what Jesus has done for you lately?" From that question alone, I was moved to write this letter.

All of you know about my biggest testimony with Surie's aneurysm and his recovery. What I also want you to know is I believe God personally chose me to help Surie through his miracle. I feel He chose me with the same hand as He chose Noah to build the ark. I know that God used the same power on me that He used on Moses to deliver His people from bondage. But he didn't use only me, but Kevin too. When we had big miracles in our family, God chose Kevin to be there for mom.

It wasn't a coincidence that Kevin just happened to be in Germany in December 1985. By Kevin being there, God had precisely set everyone in their place and answered my prayers before I even knew there was a need. To say I don't know what I would have done if Kevin were not there is an understatement.

God was so pleased with Kevin that He said, "Let's do it again!" Mother had an aneurysm ten years later. It was unreal, like déjà vu—we walked through the same hospital ward. Again, there is no other way to explain it. Mother goes to Germany and two days later she's sitting on Kevin's couch; the scene was set and the miracle began. With Mother not having medical insurance, she needed to be a dependent of someone. Kevin was the only one on active duty and she became his dependent. Mother ended up in Madigan Hospital without having the worry of paying an expensive hospital bill upon her release.

Unfortunately, there were many deaths in my immediate family's sibling set. Because I was so young when they died, I never really knew my brothers Vincent and Barron as well as I knew Alice. But what I do know about Alice is that she told me that someone prophesied that she was going to pass before the age of forty. She probably unconsciously accepted that. I also know that Alice wrote a letter to God about two weeks before she passed asking that His will be done. At the same time, David needed to be off the streets; he moved in with Alice and the scene was set.

Alice told me many times, "You are always in your right place, and whatever is supposed to be happening is happening." So if you are in your right place when miracles happen (because God is always in control), then you have to be in your right place when we perceive bad things have happened. We perceived our siblings' deaths to be a bad thing. But now I know it's not bad or good—it just is. Their deaths weren't accidents, but incidents. If Alice's death was a mistake, then a lot of things that happened in my life after her death were mistakes. Moving was based on Alice not being in Washington. California was chosen because I needed more sunshine in my life. I pray for Alice's children to blossom, just as Jennifer (Vincent's daughter) has blossomed.

Finding our home the first day I went looking was a blessing. I know having Angelina and Roger as part of our family isn't a mistake.

So what has Jesus done for me lately? Actually, I'm still receiving the afterglow from the big one. Every day is something new; this is why it is called the present time. I watched over Alice in life, and now she's watching over me in death. I give all the praise to our Almighty God! Thank you, Jesus!

Love,
Angela

CHAPTER TEN

MIRACLES IN ACTION

*"Don't define who you are and the possibilities for your life
based upon what's happening to you right now."*

Y our husband . . . he's okay . . . but he's in the hospital," the
priest at Yokota Air Force Base nervously said.

"Okay."

"Your daughter, Angela, she's okay, but she's in the
hospital."

"Okay."

The Red Cross paper continued rattling in the priest's shak-
ing hands as he read.

"Your daughter, Angelina, she's okay, but she's in the
hospital."

"Okay."

Then he took a breath. I took one too.

"Your boys, they didn't make it," he ended.

Instantly I felt as if time had stopped and no one else was in the room, just me and God. I desperately needed and wanted to hear my sons' voices.

"No, Mommy, that priest is wrong. You prayed with me 'the Lord my soul to take.' I did make it. I'm here with Jesus!" I felt I heard Murice say.

"We prayed 'the Lord my soul to take' also. I did make it. I'm here with Jesus too!" I could feel Roger say.

Somehow, their "words" instantly sent comfort through my entire mind and body. Suddenly, I could feel God's presence sending so much love and peace, there was no room for pain. The priest and my fellow soldiers stared at me, watching and waiting for my world to turn upside down. Instead, they witnessed my world in a state of complete peace, which I know could have only come from being in alignment with the One we call our Heavenly Father. I, too, was surprised.

From the small room, I called Surie's hospital room, but he wasn't in any condition to speak. However, I was able to speak with my Aunt Fedora, who was by his side. Then I was accompanied back to the dormitory, where I called Angela's room. I didn't say anything about her brothers' deaths, as my cousin Pam was going to tell her in person and hadn't done so yet. Angela's voice sounded really strong as she described to me what had happened.

∽

On April 1, 2000, after errands and the 99 Cent Store, my family's routine became everything but that. Riding center lane on the freeway, Surie and the children noticed the burgundy car in the right lane. This vehicle quickly sped past them, cut into their lane, and abruptly slowed down. Maybe the bright orange signs that read "Fines Double in Construction Zone" caught the eye of the driver.

To avoid hitting the burgundy car, Surie slammed on his brakes and swerved. Though he managed not to hit the car, the center divider was unavoidable. Upon impact everyone was knocked unconscious. Our truck bounced off the divider, moving against the flow of traffic, and then traveled backwards across three traffic lanes, hitting a six-inch curb. With no guardrails to stop its momentum, our truck—my family still inside—flipped mid-air and plummeted twenty-five feet off the freeway. It landed in the Salvation Army's parking lot below, upside down on top of two parked vehicles. The three people inside them were extremely shaken up, but, praise God, they were all right.

Officials had to use the jaws of life to cut my family out of our truck. The entire cab was completely smashed in and mangled. Murice was sitting in the backseat on the driver's side. Roger was in the center of the backseat. They were killed instantly. Angela, who was the front passenger, injured her left knee and needed ten staples. Angelina, seated behind Angela, fractured her collarbone. Surie sustained a concussion that instantly unraveled years of therapy. He started speaking in distorted phrases again and his mind and memory lapsed.

At the scene of the crash, Surie, Angela, and Angelina were in and out of consciousness and unaware of Murice's and Roger's passing. Since Angela was the first to stabilize, the police questioned her. She told them about the burgundy car that practically stopped in front of them.

"Where's your mother?" the police officer asked Angela.

"My mother's in Japan," she answered.

At this response, the officers just thought Angela had hit her head too hard and was delirious. Surie did hit his head. His speech reverted back to the same incomprehensible stage as before his brain surgery, leaving him unable to answer any of their questions about my whereabouts. The police decided a trip to our home was the proper procedure. They retrieved our address from Surie's driver's license. Meanwhile, paramedics took the six injured to two different hospitals to prevent overwhelming the staff at one emergency room.

Praise God I wasn't there when the officers rang our doorbell. With my family in three different locations, who would I have run to first, the living or the dead? Surie and Angela were taken to one hospital, Angelina to another, and Murice and Roger were either still at the scene or transported to the city morgue. In Japan, when I was told, all I could do was be still.

My neighbors thought that my being out of the country made a bad situation worse, but God knew I needed to be that far away to hear His voice. I needed that space and time to get myself together mentally, physically, and spiritually. I have learned we are always in our right place.

After the police found no one at our home, the nurses asked Angelina for the phone numbers of any family members. Angelina hadn't memorized those numbers yet, but she did know the number of her friend Amber, who lived across the street from us. Ironically, earlier that day Murice had been playing outside and passed his football to Amber's father, Isaiah. "I'll get this when I come back," Murice had told him.

But that very afternoon when Isaiah's telephone rang, the "pass" he received was news of Murice's and Roger's passing. Isaiah informed another neighbor and went to the hospital. When he arrived, the police were in the process of interrogating Surie, who was in no condition to respond.

And, as before, officials assumed drug abuse was the cause. They were eagerly willing, wanting, and impatiently waiting for the results of the blood test so they could arrest him. His drug tests came back negative. They had rushed to judgment, concluding that he was negligent and responsible for the injuries and the death of our sons. In spite of the results, the police filed vehicular manslaughter charges against Surie. No one told him of the allegations upfront, though. It would have been too much for him to process.

Word spread swiftly throughout our neighborhood and church, and both hospitals quickly filled with people. Since I was out of the country, my neighbors went on a mission to contact me. My girls knew I was in Japan but didn't have the telephone number to reach me. Surie knew the telephone number but couldn't speak or write to relay the information. This didn't stop the neighbors. Next, they desperately sought help through the Red Cross, which needed my social security number to launch a worldwide military search. My friends directed the Red Cross to the person they knew would have the numbers—my tax man. Once he provided the information, the search began.

My neighbors contacted my cousin Pam, who lived about an hour away. Once she and her husband, Ray, arrived, my neighbor Dee Dee took Pam to both hospitals. They first saw Angela and visited with her for a while. When Pam remembered she needed to get our house keys and our home security code so she and other family members would have a place to stay, she found out our house keys had been towed along with the car keys in the truck. Toward the end of their visit, Dee Dee asked Angela for the home alarm number.

"Go ask Murice. He knows it," Angela said.

Angela's response caught Dee Dee off guard. She didn't feel it was her place to tell Angela that Murice had passed; however, she didn't want to mislead her either. She needed Angela to give her the number.

"Angela, I haven't seen Murice. Can you tell me the alarm code?" Dee Dee asked again.

"No, I can't remember it right now. My head hurts. Ask Murice. He knows it by heart," she responded again.

Reporters and police officers were outside Angela's hospital room waiting for more questioning opportunities. Pam knew she needed to tell Angela that her brothers had passed before someone else did. Pam later told me she felt Angela was traumatized and saw more of the scene than she wanted to accept. She believed Angela already knew her brothers had passed and was looking for someone to confirm this. Pam finally told her. All Angela could do was cry, which left her in no condition to talk to the reporters or the police again, so the nurses sent them away.

After leaving Angela, Dee Dee and Pam visited Surie, where there were more reporters and officers. Before leaving, they attempted to get the alarm code, which proved to be another lost cause because Surie's speech and thought process were scrambled. The doctors had heavily sedated Surie to prevent the chance of seizures, but he did his best to stay awake and assist with the security code. He wrote down several numbers mixed with letters, which are not in the code, and so it didn't make any sense. He pushed imaginary buttons in mid-air as if he were standing in front of the keypad. Then he rambled off four or five different series of numbers, and after each set he would say "Beep, beep, beep." That's the sound our alarm makes when the code is input correctly. Pam didn't know whether to laugh or cry.

"Forget the alarm code. It will just have to go off," she concluded.

As with Angela, Pam knew she had to tell Surie about Murice and Roger before she left his side. Since she was emotionally drained and at a loss as to how to tell him, she prayed over her choice of words, asking for God's peace and guidance. With the calmness that God instilled in her, Pam told him. Surie cried so uncontrollably the nurses had to immediately give him a sedative.

Pam and Dee Dee retrieved the keys from the truck, arrived at our home, and opened the front door. The alarm sounded. Pam tried inputting the various sets of numerical combinations Surie had given her. None decoded the alarm and the police were dispatched. The car crash had made such news that the policemen were already aware of the whole situation and knew the ladies weren't there to burglarize our home.

Later that afternoon, Ray picked my mother up from the airport. Once Angela was released from the hospital, my Aunt Marilyn and Uncle Billy brought her home. Angelina was also ready for discharge, but because she was our foster child, she could only be released to me, Surie, or a staff member from Childhelp USA. She remained in the hospital one more day until I returned from Japan.

"I can't believe how at peace I am, how at ease I feel," I repeatedly told Sergeant Thomas.

Her new assignment was to be my escort as we traveled back to the United States the following day. She was by my side throughout all of this, and I am eternally grateful. I talked so much about being at peace, I found myself apologizing to her. At the time, I instantaneously felt the kind of peace that takes years, if ever, for some to achieve. Without my knowing, the process that led to this moment had begun years before, with God's grace and mercy. "If anything ever happened to my children, you'd have to lock me up!" I had said before.

I had every reason to lose it, and everyone expected me to. After all, I had self-prophesied it. But God had another plan for my life.

Right before we boarded the plane, I called home from the airport. My mother, Pam, family members, and neighbors were at my house and at the hospital taking care of my family. It was comforting to know that the homefront was being cared for. This additional peace allowed me to further relax and receive the next blessing.

On the ten-hour-plus plane ride directly to Los Angeles, I was thanking God that my entire family hadn't passed on and that my sons died instantly. Knowing that they hadn't suffered was comforting to me. Being absent from the body is being present with the Lord. I was thankful they weren't hooked up to a machine waiting for me to return before they passed away. My thoughts drifted to Roger.

"You know, I only call some of my foster mothers Mommy," he had told me one day while we were driving in the car alone together. Then he reached for my hand. Roger's words were a priceless gift of love and joy. It had been such a special moment, I almost had to pull off the road to compose myself. I considered it a privilege and honor to be his "Mother" and receive all the love he had stored up while waiting for a family to share it with.

Memories of Murice flooded my mind, and then I remembered the love letter he had written to his father and me. "Mom, the letter I wrote to you and dad was God resting my soul and letting you know that all is in His divine order," was the feeling I received.

I had shared the memory of this very special moment with several people. A month before the car crash, Murice ran into the house from school and shouted excitedly, "Mommy, Daddy, I wrote you a letter. I wrote you a letter!" He was in the third grade and had completed his math test early that day, which allowed time for him to write his letter.

"What do you mean you wrote us a letter? Is this a homework assignment?"

"No, I just love you."

"Honey, get the checkbook," I told my husband, laughing.

The three of us sat at the foot of our bed while I read Murice's letter aloud.

24 Feb. 00   pg 1

Dear mom and dad from Murice

You are very nice to me you help me

with my homeworek and my book reports

and other stuff. I love you because you

made me and you taught me math and

you taught me how to read a book.

You are very cool to me and I

am happy to be with you and dad.

I Love you and dad because

you taught me a lot of stuff at home

When I am older I will be taller

than then you

you will be the short one

and I will not. But you will still

be my mom and you to dad by-by

You and dad are very cool because
you and dad play a lot you and
dad been together for 19
years going on 18 years that
is good to me I am happy for you
two that you two are together
So you can be my mom and
dad can be my dad I am
glad that I am with you two
because you and dad are
nice and cool and happy
you two are the best
parents that you can ever have

by-by

At the end of Murice's incredible letter, Surie and I just looked at one another.

"Is he talking about us?" I responded.

Tears of endearment flowed down my husband's face. He went to get a tissue. I sat there holding Murice's hands.

"Do you know what this is?"

"It's a letter, Mommy!"

"It's a love letter. Thank you so much for writing down your feelings. I'm going to buy two frames and frame your letter so that I can treasure it forever."

"Mommy, buy three frames because I'm going to write you another one," he said as his eyes lit up.

Murice ran to his room. He came back ten minutes later. God knew I was going to need more help (see page 126).

We read Murice's letters before he passed, but God's handprint wasn't revealed to us until after Murice's death. The content of both letters was beyond what an eight-year-old third grader would have written.

If Murice alone had written these letters, they would have read: "Thank you for the yo-yo. Can I get a new one?" But Murice's letters were more a reflection of his loving spirit. They were to edify us, not a setup to ask for something.

He first expressed his gratitude to us for educating him. If he wasn't able to read or write, he would never have been able to give us this precious gift. And what was most important to him was the quality time we shared together.

24 Feb.00 pg2

Dear mom   from Murice

Mom you are the the best

mom you can ever a have.

If I got to choose a mom I

would choose you because

you are very very cool to

me because you are very

Smart to me. You are very

good with kids like me.

I am ghad to be here with

you, that's why I would choose

you. The mom that I got

is very cool and very fun.

by-by

"I love you and dad because you taught me a lot of stuff at home."

We taught our children about the love of God at home.

"When I am older I will be taller than you, then you will be the short one and I will not."

Currently, I am looking up to Murice, and admirably.

"But you will still be my mom and you to[o] dad."

I believe here the Holy Spirit was having Murice convey that after he passed we would still be his earthly parents.

"You and dad been together for 17 years going on 18 years."

So many parents separate or divorce after the death of a child/children. Murice's letter was saying don't even go there. You were together before I was born, and you had better stay together after I'm gone. Why? Because "that is good to me" was the message we gathered.

"If I got to choose a mom I would choose you."

This sentence is so intriguing to me. Why would someone say "If I could choose you" when they already had you? He wrote this as if he wasn't physically here. The Holy Spirit knows everyone from the beginning to the end of time. It gives me great joy to know, even with all my faults, I would still be chosen to be Murice's mother.

Murice ended all three of his pages with the words *by-by*. He knew the difference between *by, bye,* and *buy*. The Holy Spirit chose to use *by*, which means "nearby" or "close at hand." What's more, *by-and-by* implies we will see each other again at a future time.

I'm so grateful that I have this wonderful memory and God allowed Murice to write his precious letters. I will cherish them always. I thanked my son then for writing down his feelings, and I'm more proud of him today. Murice's letters were not a class assignment, but a wonderful, thoughtful, loving gift from the mighty God we serve.

Parents would like to feel they succeeded in raising their children the best they knew how. Murice's letters left us no doubt that he was pleased. They are the reason I can stand here right now with my sanity still intact. The letters reassured me that God was and is in the midst of this storm and that He orchestrates our lives. God knew Alice's letter was the answer to my hopes and prayers for peace; Murice's letters were an example of God's promises and faithfulness.

> *Now faith is the substance of things hoped for,*
> *the evidence of things not seen.*
> —Hebrews 11:1 New King James Version

∽

When Sergeant Thomas and I landed in Los Angeles, First Sergeant Sherron picked us up from the airport. For me, it was a long ride home. When we finally arrived, I went directly upstairs to recover Murice's letters from the dresser in my bedroom, where we last read them together. I read the letters aloud for everyone who was present. No one could believe Murice's particular choice of words—how profound they were and how they now took on a whole new meaning, a whole new beginning.

When I arrived home, the blinds in Murice and Roger's bedroom were already drawn and their door closed. I quickly reopened their door, raised the blinds and opened the windows, inviting the sunshine back in. I let my family know that the boys' room was still part of our home and not off-limits. If Murice and Roger were physically present, they would be out playing in those same rays of sunlight. I felt early on that I didn't want to waste weeks, months, or years of precious time not enjoying the things we had always treasured together.

I learned that reporters had gone door-to-door in my neighborhood and at my children's school asking questions for their stories. With all of the media hype that I came home to, I could have easily gotten caught up in the devil's drama and played the hysterical mama. Headlines with dramatic statements greeted me from the front pages of the local newspapers at my front door: "CRASH KILLS TWO EIGHT-YEAR-OLD BOYS," "TWO DIE WHEN TRUCK FLIPS OFF I-215," "CRASH LEAVES FAMILY DEVASTATED."

One article read: "Hours after racing home from Naval Reserve duty in Japan on Monday, Angela Alexander faced a nightmare: tending to her hospitalized husband, helping get a foster daughter released from a hospital and preparing for the burial of her son and foster son."

As you can see, the facts were not always accurate and sometimes exploited and sensationalized. The reporters were constant, but, overall, I have to say they were nice to us. The newspapers wanted to report the story, even if it wasn't factual, but God wants you to know the testimony behind the headlines, the glory behind the story.

∽

Pam took me to the hospital to get Angelina, who kept asking about Surie, Angela, and the boys. She wanted to go home to see everyone.

Pam was very concerned. "We can't let her go to the house looking for her brothers, knowing they're not there."

I took Angelina out into the hallway and gently told her Murice and Roger had died in the car crash. I don't remember the exact words that I said, but when I saw her tears, I knew she understood.

We went to see Surie. My neighbors and church members had been visiting and praying for my husband around the clock. He was asleep when we arrived, but upon hearing my voice, he awakened. As we stared at one another, tears began to flood our eyes, replacing our unspoken emotions. The words just couldn't be formed.

"Whatever you do, I do," Surie struggled to tell me, meaning, if you go crazy, I'll go crazy. If you're strong, I'll be strong. But if you die, bury me first.

CHAPTER ELEVEN

MY PEACE IS COMPLETE

"Too many of us are not living our dream
because we are living our fears."

My mother, Aunt Fedora, and Pastor Joyce Blames from my church accompanied me to the mortuary. The attendant began asking questions in preparation for Murice's wake and funeral. He couldn't guarantee there would be a wake until he determined if Murice's body was viewable, but the body was still at the morgue, due to arrive at the funeral home the following day. We were informed that the wishes of Roger's biological parents would be followed when it came to his burial arrangements.

The next morning, the attendant called and said Murice had arrived and his body was viewable. I was happy that we would be able to see Murice, but in the wee hours of the morning I had decided not to have a wake or a funeral. Instead, we started making plans for Murice and Roger's memorial service.

We also decided to cremate Murice's remains. If we buried him, we knew it would only be his body at the grave site, not his spirit, but we would still feel guilty if we didn't visit frequently, and we didn't need that dilemma. This is a very personal decision for everyone. Later we found out that Roger's remains had been cremated as well.

Aunt Fedora went back to the mortuary with me when I took Murice's clothes for his cremation. I put two pieces of candy in one of his pockets, one for him and one for his brother. Full-blown butterflies turned flips inside my stomach. I went to the bathroom at least three times while I waited to see Murice's body. I hesitated, wondering if I should have this as my last memory of my son. At the same time, I didn't want to wake up one morning regretting that I "coulda, woulda, shoulda" seen Murice.

"Conquer your fears! What would you do if you weren't afraid to fail and you knew the outcome would be a total success?" I would have said to my children. "That's how you need to approach all of your goals—have faith, focus, and follow through; pray, prepare, and stay to the end."

While we waited in the lobby of the mortuary, I desperately wanted to wake up from this dream, but it was real. Finally, the weight of knowing this would be my last chance to see Murice on earth helped me decide to move forward.

My husband would not have the chance to see our son

before he was cremated. Surie was in no condition, mentally or physically, to leave the hospital, not even for this occasion. But for me, it was either now or never.

The lady at the mortuary gave me what was left in Murice's pockets after the crash—toys, Starburst candy wrappers, and two lollipops from his visit to the 99 Cent Store and change left from the allowance he had spent. Then two attendants led my aunt and me downstairs, where we entered a small hallway. I didn't know if I imagined it or whether the temperature actually dropped a few degrees. On my right was a room separated by just a curtain. The attendant stopped to prepare us.

"Murice is behind the curtain on the gurney, covered to his neck with a sheet," she told us.

Together Aunt Fedora and I moved the curtain aside and entered the room. I glanced at the face of the body on the gurney.

"Where's Murice?" I immediately said aloud.

I looked around the small room to find him. There was no one else present but the three of us. I immediately walked out of the room, leaving the curtain swaying behind me. My aunt came out shortly after me.

"Angela, that was Murice," she said.

Then I realized my son's body was viewable but not quickly recognizable. His head was swollen. Aunt Fedora asked if I minded if she went back inside to pray over his body. I listened from behind the curtain. When she came out, I asked her to go back and pull the sheet completely over Murice. Together we reentered and I embraced my son's body from head to toe.

In fact, my only glance at Murice was so quick, I presently have no recollection of what I saw. God simply blocked it out. As we slowly walked away, again filled with peace, I felt Murice's spirit.

"You're right, Mommy. That's not me, because Roger and I are here with you."

The following day, my sister-in-law Paulette and I went to a business that specialized in urns. When we arrived at the establishment, the owner immediately put on his prepared condolence face. As we looked around, we didn't see any displays that we liked. Most of the urns were box shaped, etched with flowers, and much too old-fashioned for my young and active Murice. We looked through some of their catalogs. We searched with so much enthusiasm, the owner was puzzled by our positive behavior.

"Is the mother available?" he asked.

"I am the mother," he was surprised to hear.

We soon found the perfect urn. I was so pleased with it. It was an ocean wave crest, charcoal in color, with three gold dolphins swimming swiftly through the water. The three dolphins are a wonderful representation of Alice, Murice, and Roger, I thought—their memories united, swimming together in one monument. The urn is a permanent symbol of my three miracles in action. Murice's urn is now displayed in our home near the fireplace, where Angela, Angelina, Murice, Roger and I spent many winter evenings cuddling together and reading while waiting for the room to warm.

∽

On Valentine's Day 2000, less than two months before the death of my sons, I started a new job working at Balloon Haven. Valentine's Day was always the busiest day of the year for Ba'Loonnie Toone Lane. When I told Murice I had accepted this part-time position, he hugged me and said, "Mommy, you already work two days a month! How much can a son take?"

That was so funny to me. As you know, many parents work five days a week. Murice enjoyed coming home to both his parents, and from his letter, you can tell he didn't take us for granted. Nothing was left unsaid between the three of us. We didn't understand for a long time why Surie lived after having suffered such a severe brain aneurysm. Now we know that his survival wasn't all about him and that his unborn seed was blessed with an assignment. With Surie's early retirement, God allowed both of us to be stay-at-home parents so we could have the time and freedom to be involved in our children's daily lives. There is peace that comes from knowing that God has included us in His plan.

∽

The Thursday before Murice and Roger's memorial service, I stood in my kitchen and prayed.

Dear God, thank you so much for Murice's incredible good-bye letter. It's the reason I can stand here right now. I need to know that Roger was part of Your plan and he didn't just get caught up in Murice's homecoming. God, I simply need to know if this was Your will.

My family was watching me closely and with much concern, particularly when I began looking for some sort of farewell message from Roger. Following my prayer, God told me to search for one, but no one knew this. It didn't matter to me that people thought I had gone crazy. I started searching for a note of consolation on pure faith. I searched Roger's room, his backpack, underneath his bed. I emptied bags of school supplies and turned over couch cushions. Then I felt Pam's eyes staring at me. I love her dearly, but she's very dramatic.

"What are you doing?"

"I'm looking for something."

"I can see that, but what?"

"I don't know."

"I knew it was only a matter of time before you went crazy. Girl, you're starting to make me nervous. Why don't you lie down somewhere?"

"No, I need to find what I'm looking for."

"What is it?"

"I don't know."

"Well, is it bigger than a breadbox?"

I didn't respond.

"Okay, now I'm calling 911," she said. "Maybe they can help you find it."

I searched the house for over three hours. I didn't find a thing, but I wasn't fazed or discouraged.

As only God can create it, as only God can orchestrate it, that very evening was Open House at my children's school. Angela and Angelina were also watching my every move. If I had gone into a corner and cried, they would have followed. If I had cursed God, they would have heard. My girls needed some normalcy in their lives. The other children on our block were attending the Open House, so we left a house full of people and went as well.

My family's car crash affected almost every grade level in the elementary school. In each of our girl's classes, which we visited first, we found sincere handwritten condolence cards and letters from the students to our family.

When we entered Murice's cozy, lamp-lit class, a hush spread throughout the room. I greeted Mrs. Keltner, Murice's third grade teacher, and noticed out of the corner of my eye that the principal, Mrs. Carlmark, and assistant principal, Mrs. Peace, were standing by—each equipped with two-way radios. They were shocked and pleased that I had shown up only five days after my sons' deaths. Unbeknownst to me, Mrs. Peace was assigned to escort me on the school grounds. News reporters were still lurking. Then my eyes turned in the direction of Murice's desk.

There it was, Murice's favorite green and orange Miami Hurricanes sweater hanging on the back of his chair. Lord knows that boy was always hugged up in that jersey. As I wrapped his sweater gently over my arm, I noticed his supplies still sat in his desk. They were just the way he had left them. His classmates were very sad. They had just seen Murice on Friday, and the next day he was gone. It was hard for them to comprehend that their classmate had died. It was a moving and emotional visit for us all. For the remainder of the school year, Murice's classmates wouldn't allow any new students to occupy his desk.

We then walked to Roger's second grade classroom, where Mrs. Blassey taught. We spoke for a while, and she too gave her tearful condolences. Then my attention was drawn to an exhibit board where the students' school projects were on display. When I opened Roger's project and saw his creation, I instantly knew this was what I had been searching for. I had just prayed hours earlier that day for a memento from Roger. What I didn't know was that God had answered my prayer before I even knew I was in need.

As I read Roger's words, I nearly fell to my knees in praises to God. Murice's letter was written for the believers. If you believe in God, you can see His handprint throughout the letter. Roger's project was created for the nonbelievers.

Two weeks before the car crash, Mrs. Blassey had given her students an arts and crafts project with no specific instruction. The students were to make something to display for their parents for Open House. Well, God designed this opportunity for Roger to leave behind his incredible "good-bye" message. All the other children's projects were open faced, meaning you could see their creations from across the room. Roger constructed his project with closed doors, not to be opened or looked into until after his death.

Roger took his construction paper and cut out the shape of a house with clamps closing the double doors. Upon opening the doors in the center of the paper, this is what he wrote: *"I have a big back yard. And a big house. My mom and dad have a bathroom in theair room."*

Since we have one of the smallest backyards on our block and Roger was in transition mode, I believe he was describing his new heavenly home. On the inside flap of the door to the left of his home description, he cut out what looked like a tombstone. My eyes tried to believe it was the shape of a window frame. It also looked like one of the Ten Commandments tablets, but I couldn't deny the truth—it was the shape of a tombstone. On it he wrote, "Dead men joy." Below those words, Roger drew a little picture of himself.

On the inside flap of the adjoining door to the right side of his home description—yes, there it was again—another tombstone. He inscribed on that one "Dead men jam." Underneath those words, Roger drew a little picture of his brother, Murice, who was always dancing around the house. Roger had put two pieces of paper together, folded them in half, and cut the tombstones out at the same time. Two weeks later, they died at the same time. To me, the clamps on the closed doors represent Roger's arms, Murice's arms, Alice's arms, God's arms as they surround, caress, and continue to comfort our home. On the front of the house he drew two faces watching and smiling over us (one you can barely see). No doubt angels continuously have their arms of protection embracing our home. Eight people were involved in this car crash, but the only two people Roger wrote about were the only two people who passed. What a wonderful spiritual revelation Roger had experienced. (See picture of project, pages 144–45.)

Had Mrs. Blassey seen the tombstones, she would have been obligated to report this to the Child Protection Agency because Roger was a foster child, and our social worker would have been called in. The social worker later told us that because of the nature of Roger's project, our family would have been required to attend group therapy. Then the questioning would have begun about Roger's references to death. Thankfully, Roger wasn't questioned. What would he have said? God never placed him in the position to have to respond to any questions; his death answered all the questions concerning his project. The Holy Spirit knew beforehand that this would be the exact blessing I needed for completeness and total peace. Most people say you have to see it to believe it, but in actuality, you have to believe it in order to see it. As I searched for Roger's message, I believed and had faith that it existed, and it did.

"Dead men joy, Dead men jam," Roger wrote. Murice and Roger are joyfully jamming with Jesus!

> *And whatever you ask in My name, that will I do,*
> *that the Father may be glorified in the Son.*
> *If you ask anything in my name, I will do it.*
> —John 14:13–14

∽

Many people watched and waited for me to have a mental collapse. My neighbors didn't know about the breakdown I had experienced after my sister passed. They weren't privy to the preparations that preceded the blessings they were witnessing. The lessons I learned from Alice's death allowed me to stand strong. The strength they have witnessed from day one to the present is due to my mental breakthrough—that eternal peace that surpasses all understanding, which you can only get from God.

I felt that Murice and Roger had been prepared and were

I have a big back yard
has a big house.
My mom and dad have
a bathroom in their
room.

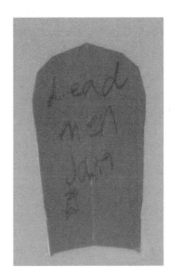

I have a big back yard.
And a big house.
My mom and dad have
a bath room in theair
room.

accepted with full scholarships into the college of their choice. It just happened to be UJC (University of Jesus Christ), and I couldn't be more excited and proud of them. Yes, I miss them dearly, but they were angels sent here on assignment. They did their job, and now they've gone off to continue doing our Father's business. "We are not human beings having a spiritual experience; we are spiritual beings having a human experience," I have read and do believe.

Several times I have heard people say, "I can't imagine what it must feel like to lose two children." I can't imagine what it must feel like to lose someone without having God in your life. So many people doubt Him, but I can't live without Him. "I can't handle my affairs without You" were Alice's words. I agree with her.

In the midst of my storm, I had so much to be grateful for. Murice's letter and Roger's project perfectly completed what the Holy Spirit had started with Alice—words of comfort that offered me a pathway to peace. I read Alice's, Murice's, and Roger's words over and over again. Still today, I get chills every time I read them. And whenever I visit the scene of the crash, I receive confirmation that God's purpose was in process. Some of my friends would drive out of their way to avoid the location where Murice and Roger passed; I made it a point to go there. Our truck didn't fall in a ditch somewhere, but, of all places, the parking lot of a Salvation Army.

Throughout this time, I learned that no one can decide for me whether the news they deliver is good or bad. The news is only information; the spin I put on it determines how it affects me and my life. After Alice died, I decided that miracles are always in action no matter how the situation may look on the surface. If God is always in control, then God is always in control. I choose to see the world not as it seems but as I am, and I am one who believes that God's plans are constantly in action, even in death.

As I was praising God daily and accepting my children's deaths, the devil tried to attack my faith with doubt. He came with his purpose, plots, and plans to kill, steal, and destroy my relationship with God. The devil tried to interfere with this miracle in action, but my faith had grown too strong to become weak.

After my sister passed, I self-destructed. After my sons passed, I mastered peace. These feelings of comfort and serenity are always with me. I've learned that with understanding comes acceptance, with acceptance comes peace, and because of my personal relationship with God, my peace is complete.

> *These things I have spoken to you,*
> *that in me you may have peace.*
> *In the world you will have tribulation;*
> *but be of good cheer,*
> *I have overcome the world.*

—John 16:33

Letters from Murice's Classmates

Dear Mrs. Alexander,

I've only known Murice for only four months. Murice was very funny. Murice loved basketball. He called himself, "The great one."

—Jacob

My memories of Murice Alexander,

I am Murice's friend, Ryan. Murice was like a brother to me. I remember how he used to give good comments about me. Murice is a good kid. He didn't deserve this to happen to him. I will always remember Murice Alexander. He was only eight years old. We'll miss you Murice, "The great one."

—Ryan

Dear Mrs. and Mr. Alexander,

Murice was a nice friend or as he called himself, "The great one." I always called him "Math Murice." Murice was a friend who was always there. For lunch when we played basketball, he would pass the ball to me.

—Alyssa

Dear Mrs. and Mr. Alexander,

Murice was the best in math, he was one of the best students in the class. Murice was like a friend who was always there, he was called "The Great One" or "Math Murice."

—Gabriella

Poems from Angela's Classmates

We are so sad
We feel so bad
We feel the pain
We know it's insane
Your brothers died
They had lots of pride
I want to cry like I got Tide in my eyes.
I feel sorrow and I wish I can see
your brothers tomorrow.
Your brothers were grateful and mostly faithful.
They played video games and they were
in the Hall of Fame.
I'm happy you're alive after that
four-wheel drive.

—Dominique

When we heard that you were there,
everybody had a great scare.
When we found out that you didn't die,
everybody in the class started to cry.
Even though your brothers are gone,
I will remember them till the break of dawn.
I know what happened to your dad,
but now he's alright makes this classroom glad.

—Ryan

Letter from David

June 4, 2000

Dear Angela,

Yes, praise the Lord for His unchanging goodness! He comforts us, and forgives us, and knows what's in our hearts. I got your letter. Thank you. I was unable to have the pictures you sent because they must have my name and D.O.C. # on the back.

The letters especially moved me that Murice and Roger wrote. They are truly expressions of pure love and intelligence for eight-year-olds. Murice was (is) a very smart boy and very loving as well. This I know even from the few times that I met him. Roger and Murice will go on to greater things with love like theirs. One glorious day, even day-by-day, we shall all witness such love.

I think of Alice often and pray. We meet in thought at times on different things like her children. Like a good and loving mother, I can see her looking over their best welfare. I love Alice dearly, and her children as well, and keep them in my most fervent prayer.

You must believe that I never consciously intended the misfortune with Alice, but anger and mental illness overcame my consciousness and the dark side of mortal fate happened. But spiritually, I've come to know that we have not been touched by mortal fate and our love goes on unbroken, and this is what's real; this is what really matters; this is what Christ reveals as our true reality and relationship with one another.

I speak with Sharon and Mother regularly on the phone and our relationship and conversations reflect love, a much needed and healing love. I have even talked with Daddy on the phone a few times recently and there is no doubt that his forgiveness, understanding, and willingness to communicate is an act and growth of love. Daddy, Mother, and Pearl (my stepmother) are planning to visit me soon and I really look forward to it.

I've been blessed to have my guitar here. I play and sing Christian songs in the Chapel services here on Sundays and it is a joy and a blessing to do so. This past Memorial Day, May 29th, (the anniversary of Alice's death), we had a concert in the big yard put on by inmates. I played and sang a couple of songs I wrote and afterwards several inmates, even some guards, came to me with compliments of my performance. I did practice but I also prayed as well and, thus, one more demonstration of God's goodness.

In your letter to the family, you spoke highly of Kevin. I too am proud of Kevin. I admire his success with his kids and his wife. I also admire Kevin for the social stability he has attained and his general achievements as an individual. You and Kevin are both, in my opinion, role models. And, even from here, I look up to the both of you.

Angela, how are little Angela, Angelina, and Surie? They enter my thoughts and prayers quite often. I see you all as being very blessed, having one another, and nothing could be much better than that.

Well, I'll close for now and wish you, Angela, your family, and our family, health, happiness, peace, understanding and love.

Love,
David

> *For God so loved the world that He gave His only begotten*
> *Son, that whoever believes in Him should not perish*
> *but have everlasting life.*

—John 3:16

My U.S. Air Force basic training photo, Lackland AFB, Texas, 1982.

Surie, a true soldier, proudly displays his U.S. Army uniform, 1984.

My siblings at a Thanksgiving dinner gathering, 1986: (front row, left to right) Angela (me), Susan, and Alice; (back row) Barron, Sharon, and Kevin.

Surie and I vacationing in Hawaii, 1987.

Angela, Lareina, Murice, and Arsenio, 1991.

Wedding photo of my mother, Julia, sixteen years old, 1950.

My brother David, 1981.

Our new neighborhood—Rome Jr., Arsenio, Murice, and Dominique, 1999.

Angela, Surie, and Murice, 1997.

Alice (right) and I enjoying a luau in Hawaii, 1987.

Murice Tayes Alexander on graduation day from Dee and Dora's Daycare, June 1996, Tacoma, Washington.

Family gathering (from bottom, left to right): Matthew, Joshua, Arsenio, Murice, Angela (me), Steve, Susan, Angela, Lovell, Julia, Alice, and Lareina, May 1996.

CHAPTER TWELVE

A PEACE BIGGER THAN ME

*"If you put yourself in a position where you
have to stretch outside your comfort zone,
then you are forced to expand your consciousness."*

We wanted the last visual memory of Murice and Roger to be of them playing basketball, football, and riding their bikes. I wanted it to be a celebration of their lives, especially since so many of their friends would be in attendance.

For three nights, I stayed up until after 2 a.m. in preparation for my sons' memorial service. Each night, I woke up after only two hours of sleep and worked on a eulogy and a good-bye letter to both of my sons. Then I would doze off again until about 6 a.m.

As I wrote, I could hear Murice's and Roger's spirits telling me, "Write this, Mom" and "Remember that, Mommy." I also heard God reveal to me that Alice's, Murice's, and Roger's messages were written not only to soothe my soul but, more

share with the world. Oh no, here's my mission,
　　　　　rself. We all have an assignment here on earth,
and I struggled with mine.

"I'm not a writer or a public speaker. This is outside of my comfort zone," I said to God.

"This is not about you! It's about the people this testimony will bless and comfort," God told me.

I wish I could tell you that I was submissive right away, but that's not my testimony. I knew the story was worthy to be told, but I walked in disobedience for five months because I doubted myself. This time wasn't pleasant or easy for me. God disrupted my schedule; He took my peace and appetite away until my obedience became mandatory. I finally decided I wasn't going to allow my comfort zone to turn my desires into my excuses. I surrendered and decided to bet on myself instead of against myself. I know what God ordains He maintains, and when God gives you a vision, He's already made the provisions, and when your vision is clear your resources will appear. However, I did ask God for an Aaron, as Moses had done. He told me, "The Holy Spirit is your Aaron." With that, I responded, "God, as long as You lead me, I'll be Your willing vessel." From then on, my daily affirmation became "I am an international, inspirational, successful dynamic speaker."

Before God gives you an assignment, He already knows your ability. The question is, are you available? As members of the body of Christ, we have a human body only because we have a heavenly purpose to fulfill on earth. As the scripture tells us, our future is God's history: "You saw me before I was born. Every day of my life was recorded in your book. Every moment was laid out before a single day had passed." (Psalm 139:16)

Next to me, Pam tried to sleep, but each morning before sunrise I awakened her with my shuffling papers. My cousin seriously thought I had gone crazy when she heard me talking to myself. After I finished writing, I would lie still, close my eyes and listen for the slightest sound of movement around the house. I could always count on Clara to be the first one up. My mother would awaken shortly after. Then I would arise to tear-stained pillows and begin my day talking with my elders, gathering bits of wisdom and prayers to prepare me and give me strength for the day.

My physical needs were met spiritually. I barely ate or slept, but I was neither tired nor hungry. During this time, I did what came naturally. I started my list of things I needed to do. Whatever I needed, big or small, prayers went up and blessings came down. When my church needed pictures of Murice and Roger for the front of the memorial service program, I had no fitting pictures, only videotapes. That very day Mrs. Carlmark and Mrs. Peace came to visit. Along with their condolences, they brought the school pictures that Murice and Roger had taken just two weeks prior. When I needed stockings for the service and didn't have time to go to the store, my daughter Angela discovered that the mailman had just delivered sample stockings to our mailbox—my exact size and color. These are just a couple of examples of the countless miracles that were in action.

Sergeant Thomas was still right by my side at my home to help me stay organized. She greeted each visitor with her professional military demeanor.

"Girl, how did you get a military secretary?" family and friends would ask. In the military, you need to go through a chain of command to get such a benefit, but when God's involved, there's no protocol.

Our home wasn't the place for a pity party, just the opposite. There was a definite sense of tranquility that all was in order, and peace comforted all who entered. Just as Roger's project portrayed, our home exuded warmth, as if surrounded by loving arms.

The letter I sent my family two months before now took on a special meaning. It prepared them to see me. Now my family prayed I would have the faith to walk my written talk. Even though my niece Jennifer hadn't responded to my letter, she was moved to share it with her family and friends. When she came to California for the service, she brought her well-read copy of the letter with her in case she needed to refresh my memory that my struggle with death was complete. She was so happy to see that my talk was demonstrated by my walk. A lot of Christians praise God when everything is good, but the true level of our belief is demonstrated when our faith is tested.

Since I knew it was better to prepare than repair, I chose this period to maintain an "attitude of gratitude" journal. I simply knew the more good you look for, the more good you will find. Tony and Sheila Marchbanks, former directors of our marriage ministry, have reminded us of this: "The choice is yours whether your life's testimony is going to be of grace or of grievances."

I didn't know what tomorrow would hold, but I did know Who holds tomorrow. I understood that thoughts turn into words and that words can turn into reality. The seeds that I sowed now would be the harvest that my family and I would reap in the future. Now is always a good time to lay down the foundation for your family's godly heritage for generations to come.

I have heard many times, "Wherever you find yourself, you made the appointment to be there" and "The best way to predict your future is to create it." So I knew I had to focus on the positive in order to have a favorable outcome. It would have been easier for me to simply curl up and give up. But when you know better, you should do better, and I knew I needed to ensure a solid structure for my personal road to recovery. With the lessons learned from Alice's death, I knew the pathway to my peace was through the Holy Spirit. Already I could feel my road to recovery wouldn't be as winding as before.

Death and life are in the power of the tongue,
and those who love it will eat its fruit.

—Proverbs 18:21

〜

On the day of Murice and Roger's memorial service, Surie received a day's pass from the VA hospital. Although Pam had told Surie of the boys' passing, the magnitude of this news was still too difficult for him to comprehend. Because the concussion Surie suffered in the car crash caused a serious setback to the progress he had made following his brain aneurysm, grieving the death of his sons was a concept far too great for his mind to process or accept.

My brother Kevin and Sergeant Daniel escorted Surie from the hospital to our home. As their car approached our neighborhood's familiar surroundings, Surie's anxiety heightened. No one could predict what his reaction would be. Exiting the car was both a laborious and emotional task. With Kevin and Daniel's support, Surie headed toward the entrance of our home.

Our front door opened to reveal Murice and Roger's memorial posters still being readied. Greetings gave way to inquiry as he pondered the presence of out-of-town relatives, the bustle of preparation, and the reality of the moment. At last, the processing began. It was obvious Surie needed a moment to collect his thoughts. He surveyed the living room for signs of his boys, their laughter, their faces—them. Yet there wasn't time to let everything sink in. We needed to give immediate attention to getting Surie dressed for the service. This necessary task provided only a temporary distraction, for the emotions were yet to come. In fact, as Kevin escorted Surie through the house and up the stairwell, Surie's awareness heightened with each step he took.

With each step, gravity and grief weighed upon Surie, who had already been weakened by denial. As our second-story landing came into view, Surie mustered up the strength to navigate the remaining stairs only to find himself facing our sons' bedroom. The moment had come for him to deal with the silent and motionless room that was once filled with the joyous sounds of his two vivacious eight-year-old sons. In this moment, he could deny it no more. He could no longer hide behind the numbing medication.

Surie broke down right there. With so much activity going on downstairs, only Kevin and I experienced this private moment with Surie. Weakened by despair, he collapsed. Seeing my strong husband buckle under the pressure of grief, I knew that only God had the strength to lift him spiritually. Kevin and I did our best to physically carry him to our bedroom, where Surie cried incessantly.

Kevin helped Surie get dressed, Daniel cut his hair, and I put the finishing touches on the essential details for the service.

As the family busied themselves and organized the vehicles for the caravan to the service, the Bereavement Ministry from our church came to prepare our home for the repast. Throughout all the preparations, I remained calm and simply took care of what needed to be done.

As the caravan made its way to the church, my mind went through its internal checklist. Little things like the balloon bouquet and friends and family being able to find the church on time concerned me. As I approached the church grounds, I saw many cars lining the streets and filling the parking lot, eventually to capacity. An entourage of well-wishers waited to greet my family as we arrived.

Many of the greeters seemed to look in my eyes for answers. Some searched for the right words to say. For others, it was easier to avoid me altogether. They were confused by my uplifted spirit. They hadn't seen my letters. They hadn't experienced my blessings. They didn't know how God had prepared me for this day. They simply weren't aware of my testimony.

While I knew my boys had touched many hearts, I hadn't realized until the moment I entered the sanctuary that Murice and Roger also affected so many other lives. The church was filled with relatives; church members; friends; my military family, dressed in their blues; and a host of unfamiliar faces. Some of the people I had never met before. They knew my sons or simply came because they heard about their deaths.

During the service, I sat and watched three days of preparations unfold beautifully. Smiling faces of Murice and Roger were captured on pictures displayed on the easels. Not only were there balloon bouquets, but Balloon Haven had also brought two beautiful balloon-sculptured crosses with big blue bows with the boys' names attached in gold lettering.

My pastor, Diego Mesa, set a calm and pleasant atmosphere by starting the service with a prayer. He informed the congregation that I had named the day MIA (Miracles in Action). Next, the children's choir sang. As I listened, I imagined Murice's and Roger's voices joining in perfect harmony with the other children. My Aunt Marilyn and Uncle Billy, formerly lead singers in The Fifth Dimension, also sang two songs, "Keep the Love Light Burning" and "The Love of God," which brought the house down.

"It's not the duration of Murice's and Roger's lives, but the donation of their lives," Pastor Diego revealed.

Mrs. Keltner, Murice's teacher, with Mrs. Peace by her side for support, read the "by-by" letters Murice had written. Sergeant Reginald Daniel presented and explained Roger's "Dead men joy, Dead men jam" project. Then a host of family and friends expressed their feelings about my sons. Tears flowed while Murice's and Roger's schoolmates and their neighborhood friends spoke words that touched our hearts. Angela, being the shining star that she knows she is, shared funny memories of her brothers. I was so proud of her. She didn't get nervous in the service or miss the moving moment. Rita Merchant, one of our church soloists, sang Patti LaBelle's "Love Never Dies," the song that brought so much healing to my soul after Alice's death. Then Lenard Knight sang "Jesus Loves the Little Children."

I'm so blessed to have personally known Murice and Roger. To be honored with the gift of being their mother was simply my pleasure. I love them both. I wrote Murice's eulogy, and Roger's previous foster mother, Charlotte Beamon, wrote Roger's. While we were gathering the facts, we discovered that both boys had given their lives to God at the young age of five. At the time, they lived in different states and hadn't yet physically met, but their spirits were already in sync. Pastor Diego read their eulogies.

I sat through it all—each song, a source of strength, each letter, a legend of love, each tear, a testimony to tell.

Afterward, Surie and I greeted everyone who gathered in a receiving line of love. It was so beautiful and overwhelming that Surie could not continue standing. About a half hour into the receiving line, Rome Jr., one of Murice and Roger's closest neighborhood friends, came forward to greet us. Time stood still when I embraced him with a deep motherly hug. It felt as though Murice and Roger were hugging me back.

The flowers were gathered, taken to my home, and given out to my family and neighbors. Following the memorial service, the repast turned into a block party. While our home was packed with people, I spent hours upstairs telling friends of the many testimonies I had experienced since my sons' deaths.

Even though Surie didn't want to return to the hospital, he had to. The doctors had ordered him to check in by seven that evening. I did not want him to go either, but he needed rest after one of the most emotional days of his life. He would never have rested at our home. A few neighbors didn't leave until after two in the morning.

"This is the best day of my life!" I heard myself say, which was strange but true. How could the day of my children's memorial service be the best day of my life? I can't explain it. This peace is much bigger than me. I'm just grateful I have it!

Trust in the Lord with all your heart, and lean not on your own understanding; in all your ways acknowledge Him, and He shall direct your paths.

—Proverbs 3:5–6

CHAPTER THIRTEEN

DECIDING TO FLY

*"Just because fate doesn't deal you the right cards,
it doesn't mean you should give up. It just means you have to
play the cards you get to their maximum potential."*

Due to the concussion that reinjured Surie's brain, doctors sent him to the acute head injury unit of the VA hospital in Palo Alto in Northern California. My Aunt Maxine and Uncle Ronald lived just twenty minutes away and invited me to stay with them. The girls stayed behind. Angela was left in my mother's care at our home. According to our foster agency's guidelines, Angelina was required to go to another foster home until Surie and I returned.

While at the hospital, Surie and I celebrated what would have been Murice's ninth birthday, May 2, 2000, by releasing three balloons in the sky. That same afternoon while Surie was in therapy, I sat outside—only one month after my sons had passed—and was able to say out loud: "Murice is dead. Roger is dead." It had taken me more than a year after Alice's death to say those words. I had learned another lesson from my sister's death: express pain, release it, let go and let God. As I sat there, I wrote and vocalized a poem entitled "Out Loud."

Out Loud

Murice is dead,
Roger is dead,
my sons are dead.

I can say Roger is dead, as I sit on his bed,
Roger is dead.

I can say Murice is dead, without a tear to shed,
Murice is dead.
Roger is dead.

You see, I can say Murice is dead,
because I know where he is led.
Murice and Roger are dead.
Did you hear me?
That's what I said!

On Easter Sunday, as many celebrated Jesus' rising from the tomb, Surie rose from his hospital bed to enjoy a one-day pass outside the hospital. We went to the movies, out to dinner, and to the mall. Walking through the mall proved both humorous and embarrassing. Surie lost his peripheral vision in both eyes after the crash. As a result, he walked into fixtures and people.

"Sorry, I had a brain aneurysm, then I was in a car crash...," he tried to explain to a mannequin.

People began to stare and point. I finally had to interrupt his conversation in mid-sentence. "Baby, you don't have to apologize to the mannequin. She's not real. Look, this one doesn't even have ears or a head," I whispered to him.

"Sorry," he said again to the mannequin.

∽

Over a month later, Surie was released from Palo Alto VA Hospital and became an outpatient at our local VA Medical Center for much-needed speech therapy sessions. We came home to a stack of condolence cards and a separate pile of bills. The medical invoices were due upon receipt, therefore already late. There was one particular statement from Ambulance Medical Response (AMR) totaling over $1,400 for taking Surie and Angela only six miles to the hospital. As I stared at the invoice, I searched for the good. I soon became thankful for the bill itself. You see, there was no ambulance called for Murice and Roger. Then I noticed the letterhead with the abbreviation AMR in bold letters. From now on in this book, AMR will stand for Alice, Murice, and Roger.

While going through a pile of bills, I noticed an envelope from a life insurance agency. I didn't know what it was about, so I opened the letter. My eyes raced down the page faster than I could comprehend the written words. Then I recalled that one Thursday night, a week before I left for Japan, a phone solicitor had called. I was very busy that evening, in the middle of preparing my children for their series of Friday tests. I told the caller I couldn't talk right now and hung up the telephone.

The night before I left for Japan, the solicitor called back. Again I was busy, this time packing. But I didn't want to brush her off as before, so I listened to her spiel. She was selling accidental death insurance through my credit card company. It cost $7.95 a month to cover the cardholder and $9.95 a month for the family-plan rate.

"No, but thank you," I declined.

"Wait! We pay the first three months' premium. Within the next month, you will receive your policy. If you still don't want it, cancel, and you haven't paid anything," she asserted.

This lady was good at her job, not pushy, but persistent.

"Okay, give me the family plan," I said quickly in the middle of packing and checking homework. That was basically it. The phone call, which was less than five minutes, was over. The caller already had my personal information from my credit card records, and accidental death insurance didn't require any medical background checks.

The letter I was now reading was the insurance policy I had initiated with that call. Still, I thought that if my family was covered, the policy probably would not have taken effect right away. But I kept reading. I could hardly believe my eyes. Family coverage began April 1, 2000, the same day Murice died! You can see how God used this solicitor. He knew I had a need and sent an earthly angel to do His will. Even though I tried to end the call, the solicitor persisted.

After tithing a percentage of the insurance payout, there was still enough money to pay for all of Murice and Roger's memorial expenses. God is good! There are no coincidences or accidents. This was another confirmation from our Almighty God that He is in control, always and forever, from the beginning to the end, whether you believe it or not. God came through right on time, not a day late or a dollar short.

∽

Many people look for signs left by their loved ones after they have passed. Some may have gotten their personal affairs in order or recently completed a project. In addition to Murice's and Roger's messages, there were other notable occurrences that tied up some loose ends in my sons' lives.

Murice had a personal goal of becoming Student of the Month, like his sister Angela. The December before he passed, he and I sat down with his teacher, Mrs. Keltner, to discuss his wishes and develop a plan to achieve his goal. Since Murice had a habit of rushing through his classwork to play inside the tepee in their classroom, I used tough love and made the tent off-limits to my son. It was hard for me to stand my ground when his eyes began to water, but I did. And he rose to the challenge.

I homeschooled my children for two hours a day during that Christmas vacation. Each had a different subject to improve upon. Murice worked hard on his math. As soon as school resumed, his efforts began to pay off. By February, Murice became Student of the Month. He was so proud of himself! By March, Murice exceeded his goal. While everyone else in the class was on multiplication, he had graduated to division. His classmates soon called him "Math Murice." I was so happy and excited for him. After Murice's passing, his teacher told me he had succeeded in maintaining the number-one math score in her class for the rest of the school year.

∽

"Mommy, my last foster home was up the street," Roger excitedly said one day as we drove home. "Turn right, then right again, and it's on the left-hand side of the street before you get to the cul-de-sac." He spoke with such assurance and certainty that I immediately pulled over and stopped the car.

"What, Roger? Are you sure?" I asked him.

Roger loved his previous foster family, and his biological

sister continued to live with them. We weren't that far from our home. I had no idea Roger once lived so close to us. He was sure that this was where they lived, and he wanted to visit.

I wanted to call first, but we didn't have the family's telephone number. We took a chance. I followed the directions Roger had described. Lo and behold, he was right. We were there. I told Angela, Angelina, and Murice to stay inside the car. Roger and I got out, rang the doorbell, and stood back. I nervously prayed that strangers wouldn't answer the door and break Roger's heart. The total opposite happened.

"Rogerrrr!" screamed his previous foster mother.

His sister and everyone greeted him with hugs and kisses. It was a wonderful family reunion. My other children joined us, and we stayed there for several hours that day.

During our visit, we found out their family led a praise and worship dance group that performed for a variety of churches. They practiced every Saturday. Angela asked if she could join the dance group, and she did. So after my family's weekly Saturday errands and visit to the 99 Cent Store, we took Angela to dance practice. During rehearsals, Roger reconnected with his extended family and spent precious time with his sister before he passed. God set us up for a beautiful blessing.

∽

Angela, Angelina, Surie, and I spent the rest of the year adjusting to Murice and Roger's absence. We missed the sounds of their jumping down four to five steps at a time and then hitting the wall, the wrestling, the glow-in-the-dark yo-yos, the basketball and football playing in the house—the normal things that used to get them in trouble. We missed all those familiar sights and sounds. What's sad is that as the years pass, we often forget the small details, like facial expressions, gestures, and habits, of our loved ones—the little things we never think we will miss until the void appears.

Some routines I couldn't bear to continue. Quizzing my children on their spelling words every school night was one of many. With only Angela and Angelina at the table, it was just too painful to maintain. Since the girls already had such a good foundation in this area, they were able to test one another. Christmas was also difficult. Throughout the years, I have kept a video library of my children opening presents on Christmas morning. Christmas of 2000 I couldn't bring myself to take even one photograph because I wanted no recollections of Christmas without Murice and Roger.

When talking with a new group of friends, the question of children would often come up. "How many children do you have?" someone would ask. My tears sometimes started to fall before it was even my turn to speak. I haven't learned yet how to answer that particular question. It depends upon the situation and whether I feel comfortable talking about my sons. If I don't, I'll answer, "I have two daughters." Then the conversation continues. But I feel uneasy inside when I don't acknowledge my sons, as if they never existed. Even though I'm at peace with Murice's and Roger's passing, at times my human emotions still arise.

For a while, when Murice's and Roger's friends would walk past our home, I could hardly speak. I would get a lump in my throat from just seeing them. Dominique and Rome Jr. had grown so tall, and I wondered if Murice would have had his growth spurt as well. I pondered if Roger would have been an Alexander through adoption. I imagined what my sons might have looked like as they matured from boys to young men.

∽

My brother-in-law Steve wrote a poem when his father passed. While I read it, tears flowed, as I immediately began reminiscing and missing all of my loved ones who had passed. It reminds us of how important it is to express our love to our family while they are still with us.

Happy Father's Day

by Steven V. Banks

I woke up this morning with no one to call;
My eyes misted over, tears started to fall.
No one to listen to, nothing to say,
No celebration, not this Father's Day.

He never walked an easy road,
Uphill each step with a cumbersome load.
Me being rotten, unable to soar,
I should have lightened his load, but I added much more.

Then suns rose and set, and we grew apart,
Only in distance, not at all in our hearts.
We did miss each other, though we acted so tough,
Not telling the other, I love you! enough.

My father ran one heck of a race;
He deserves to be in a far better place.
I'll press on without him, I'll stumble, I'll fall,
For I woke up this morning with no one to call.

∽

April 1, 2001, my annual tour was at Hickam AFB, Hawaii. I struggled with the time frame because I would be away from my family on the first anniversary of our sons' deaths. As I thought about this, my mind flashed back to an experience I had when I was a little girl. After my neighbor's son passed, she spent every birthday, holiday, and anniversary of his death crying all day long. She was so loud, I could hear her from across the street. I recognized my recollection of this as a message I needed to heed: don't turn the anniversary of a loved one's death or the holidays spent without them into holler-days.

I needed to conquer my fear of leaving my family before it grew stronger and dominated my thoughts. I needed to know I could leave them home and that they would be all right no matter what date it was. If I allowed this fear to continue, when would it end? After I struggled with this decision for a day, I shook it off. I got off of my blessed assurance, hurried up, and got right before I got left.

"Hello, Aloha!" I said to my next destination.

The rest of my family faced their own challenges. Angela expressed her sadness, anger, and survivor's guilt by writing poems. She questioned why her life was spared in the crash. Even though she wouldn't let anyone see her cry, at night I heard her pain. She titled this poem "Why":

Why

by Angela T. Alexander

Why is the sky still blue?
Why do the birds continue to fly?
Why won't my wings re-spread,
and just fly high?

It feels like I'm paralyzed from the neck down.
I can't make a move
or a decent frown.

I don't know why,
my wings decided not to fly.
They were green, blue,
yellow and pink,
all made out of the rarest mink.

But,

sometimes when I daydream,
my wings spread to the extreme,
where my brothers take me on the highest swing!

Concentrating in school became quite difficult for her at times. Before the crash, Angela was an A student. After the crash, her grade point average fluctuated drastically. At one time it dropped to an all-time low of a few Cs on her progress reports. The sad thing was she no longer cared about her grades or receiving Student of the Month awards. At home, she hosted major pity parties in which she was the guest of honor. Because misery loves company, she tried her best to pull me into her depression sessions. She made mention that Murice's letters weren't addressed to her. She didn't understand and wasn't interested in my place of peace.

"God has a plan for your life. I don't know what it is, but I know He saved you for a reason," I told my children and Surie too.

"As long as you place God first in your life, there are no

limits to your achievements. Once you realize that wallowing in self-pity is of no use or value to anyone, especially yourself, your healing will begin," I consoled her.

Angela grew tired of hearing my admonishments. Gradually, her pity parties dissipated, and she blossomed again and resumed some of her former interests.

I wrote "ANGELA, BEST ACTRESS" on a big gold star and placed it on her bedroom door. We need to speak it as if it were. A local Children's Theatre Experience was presenting the play "Annie." Angela auditioned for a leading role and earned the part of a feisty character named Pepper. Her performance was outstanding. When she tried out for her school's cheerleading team, she practiced her jumps and ear-to-ear smile daily in the mirror. Her biggest smile came when she made the team. During these extracurricular activities, Angela soared academically once again. After mastering a series of tests, she was asked to join her school's academic pentathlon team.

"I'm soooo proud of myself!" she declared.

And everyone in the household would respond, "Angela, we are soooo proud of you too!" In our home, instead of getting money for good grades, our children would proclaim that phrase and receive our praises in return.

When Angela was in the fifth grade she was diagnosed with scoliosis and fitted for a back brace. The brace was so uncomfortable and embarrassing, she frequently neglected to wear it. As a result, when she was in seventh grade she became a candidate for back surgery. Doctors attached and fused rods to both sides of her backbone to correct her spine. The operation was a success, and she moves about fine now. Her situation reminded me of when I didn't wear my corrective shiny red shoes.

By the time Angelina was eight, she had already encountered so much in her young life. She had been separated from her parents, siblings, and other foster families. After the deaths of Murice and Roger, she immediately went into denial—the survival mode she had developed from past experiences. We talked about the boys daily and continued to sing "Love Never Dies." Eventually she found more comfort in talking about her emotions than in suppressing them.

I encouraged her as well to embrace the second chance at life that she had been given. I placed a big gold star on her bedroom door with the words "ANGELINA, TOP MODEL." She had dreams, and the height, to become a runway model.

Heartbreaking and sad best describes Surie's life after the crash. If he had just taken another route or left five minutes later that day, our boys would still be alive, he thought. He felt responsible and would tell me daily that all he wanted to do was die. He would also often talk to me about desperately wanting to have another baby. He simply wanted to fill that gaping hole in his heart.

"Why couldn't I have died instead of my sons? I shouldn't have even survived the aneurysm!" he would say.

His injuries compounded his emotional pain. With no peripheral vision, he lost the driving privileges he had worked so hard to regain. His speech deficiency made communicating so frustrating that at times his discord turned into depression, and his depression into withdrawal. For days he would not talk to us at all. Normally, Surie is such a friendly and fun people person. This new behavior went against the natural grain of his warm personality. Our children, especially, found him difficult to live with. Surie once loved singing in our church choir, which was easier for him to do than speaking, but now felt he didn't deserve to rejoice in praise and worship. He couldn't seem to stay involved with anything for a long period of time and found or created ways and reasons to withdraw, self-sabotage, or simply quit.

I realized that my husband's healing would occur one day at a time. We worked on his grief in therapy sessions and at home, and he worked hard to improve his speaking skills once again. I supported and encouraged him every step of the way and I tried to help him see the light ahead.

The community honored our sons by planting a tree at the new elementary school built in our neighborhood. During the school's grand opening dedication, teachers and staff from our sons' school presented our family with a beautiful plaque. It read:

On This Special Occasion a Tree Was Planted
To Celebrate the Lives of
Murice Tayes Alexander and Roger Lamont Stevens
Two Boys Who Loved to Climb to Great Heights
And Watch Over Their Loved Ones from Above.

We had more to celebrate that day. Angela turned twelve and Angelina got a present that had been five years in coming. Her biological sister, Felicity, came to live with us. After five years of separation, the sisters were ecstatic about living together again. Because of the car crash, we were nearly denied this privilege. We were under a routine investigation with the foster care system regarding Angelina's safety and Roger's death, and they placed a freeze on our home that prevented any other children from being assigned to us. In addition, the county had considered removing Angelina. The only reason they didn't carry through with this mission was that there wasn't any negligence on our part. Based on this and a favorable home visit, the county decided to make an exception and allow Felicity to live with us. Their goal was to have siblings reside together whenever possible.

The minute I found out that Felicity had dreams of being a singer, I placed a big gold star on her bedroom door that read "FELICITY, #1 SINGER." Full of raw talent, she has a beautiful voice and a wonderful gift for drawing. It's no coincidence that she was eight years old when she came to live with us—the same age my sons "left" our home. Felicity was a tomboy and replenished our home with the noise that only another eight-year-old could bring.

I know that God's desires for us are so much grander than we can ever imagine, to the point that our dreams don't begin to compare to what He has planned for us. The desires of your heart are dreams to you, but reality to God. The question is, do you trust Him, even when nothing makes sense? Yes, we're disappointed when our plans don't happen within the allotted time we scheduled. But wouldn't you rather have it done right than tonight?

CHAPTER FOURTEEN

TRIALS, TRIBULATIONS, AND TRIUMPH

*"Other people's opinion of you
does not have to become your reality."*

Our insurance agency was very understanding and helpful throughout this whole ordeal. They were amazed because our truck flipped upside down in mid-air and my family should have been pulled to the roof of the cab when the truck hit the ground. From the pictures the insurance company took, my agent could see that the entire cab of the vehicle was completely compressed so that it was level with the bed of the truck. Where was my family? The steering wheel was bent and touching the driver's seat. No one should have survived.

"For three people to walk away is truly a miracle," my agent said. Praise God that He supernaturally supersedes all laws of gravity and logic!

Just like the metal from the car crash, the pending charges and lawsuits were mangled and messy. Sorting through guilt and innocence proved a long and laborious task. I knew the vehicular manslaughter allegations were false. The charges compounded the stress my family was already under, but we remained strong, believing victory would prevail. There's a saying, "If you're going to worry, don't pray. If you're going to pray, don't worry." We prayed that Surie would be tried in truth. We prayed that when all the evidence was reviewed, he would be totally cleared. We knew God to be in the blessing business, and He continued to abundantly shower us with His love.

We were also being sued by the people in the cars that our truck fell on. One of the parties, a woman and her daughter, settled quickly. But the other lady sought $1.7 million in damages. She claimed her knee was injured. My lawyers discovered evidence that revealed a history of slips and falls as well as an x-ray of the lady's knee that was dated three days before the crash. At the time of the crash, she was in the process of filing a workmen's compensation claim at her job, but then she switched the blame to us. I'm sure the car crash aggravated her knee condition, but it was not the initial cause, as she was claiming. The woman was very sympathetic regarding the death of our children and said Caltrans, who is responsible for California's highways, owed us an apology, but that's where her condolences ended.

For years, we tried to settle with her, but the idea of

millions kept dancing in her head. Year after year, the strength of her claims grew weaker. Our position was that if the State of California and Caltrans had had a guardrail in place at the twenty-five-foot drop, our truck would not have fallen over the cliff. A week after Murice's and Roger's deaths, a guardrail was placed there. Our lawyers advised us to countersue the State of California and Caltrans for wrongful death, pain, and suffering. Unfortunately, Surie was unable to be of much assistance with our case. With his memory loss and speech disorder, he could not answer specific questions. This was probably best for him, given his state of mind.

Reliving the crash was hard on everyone. At the time of the crash, Angela testified that the burgundy car sped past the truck and then cut in front of Surie. The police thought she might have been coached. From whom and when, I wanted to know. I was in Japan, and Surie was mentally deficient. Angela's statement wasn't rehearsed and, to this day, remains the same. The driver behind Surie confirmed that the phantom burgundy car was fairly close to our truck. This witness then saw our truck swerve to the left, bounce off the guardrail, and fall off the highway.

"It happened so fast, it was as if their truck was just lifted off the road," the witness said.

The phantom car continued on and left the scene. Whether or not the driver knew what had happened, we'll never know.

This person disappeared into the traffic forever. If he had stopped, he would have been sued. But this whole ordeal wasn't really about him, but about the miracles in action.

Officials questioned Angela about the phantom car's brake lights. Based on what she said, at first I thought the brake lights were simply out. However, the investigation revealed that the cars were so close, Angela could not have seen anything below the car's rear window.

During the four years prior to our case coming to trial, we relived the details of the crash. We learned about reports from the police's and coroner's offices that we would have preferred to avoid. Depositions frequently lasted three to four hours, and I was required to respond to many pages of questions relating to our personal history, some of which were dated more than twenty years earlier.

The Los Angeles County Department of Children's Services also launched an investigation of my family in regard to Angelina's injuries. Every foster child has an attorney, and Angelina's attorney sued us on her behalf. I understood that he was doing this in Angelina's best interest, but on top of being charged with vehicular manslaughter, being sued by the lady whose car our truck landed on, and Caltrans stating that the crash was Surie's fault, Angelina's lawsuit was almost more than we could bear.

Four years after the crash, in May 2004, the courts were ready to hear our case. Murice's birthday, May 2, was on a Sunday that year. He would have been thirteen. With everything going on, my husband was so depressed that morning, he couldn't bring himself to get out of bed. Through God's grace I made it to church. My mind wandered between Murice's birthday, his death-day, and the pressure of the upcoming trial. As I sat in silence during marriage ministry class, streams of tears flowed from my eyes. Flo, one of our intercessory prayer warriors, pulled me aside into the adjoining room. After I shared with her all I was going through, she called in Opel, another powerful prayer warrior. We discussed Murice and Roger and how they are joyfully jamming with Jesus. We also prayed heavily over the trial, judge, attorneys, jurors, and the final outcome. We claimed victory in advance and gave all the glory to our almighty God.

> *Do not be afraid nor dismayed because of*
> *this great multitude, for the battle is not yours, but God's.*
> —2 Chronicles 20:15

ରୁ

A few days before the trial, the lady with the knee injury withdrew her lawsuit and settled. Her only other option would have been to commit perjury, lie on the witness stand about her injuries, and likely lose her case altogether.

On Wednesday, the first day we entered the courtroom, twenty or so double-stacked boxes of paperwork greeted us.

At first glance, that huge amount of evidence, gathered by the opposing attorneys, looked disturbing until the Holy Spirit told me it was just there to intimidate us. With that insight, I became tickled over the thought of someone having to haul those heavy boxes in and out of the courthouse every day. However, this insight did not negate the seriousness of the situation. These preliminary hearings decided which motions would be granted, which, in turn, would determine the evidence the jurors would hear.

Attorneys on both sides fought hard to have their motions approved. Our attorneys wanted to see quite a few of the Caltrans attorneys' motions denied. First, the Caltrans attorneys argued that because Surie had a history of seizures, he probably had one at the time of the crash.

The judge responded that that motion was fine to argue as long as Caltrans had a physician who would testify that Mr. Alexander caused the crash because he was having a seizure. They didn't have a doctor to validate that claim because it wasn't true. I'm sure they mentioned it to plant a tainted seed in the jurors' minds. Plus, it would have forced our attorneys to have to prove that Surie didn't have a seizure. Their first motion was denied.

Secondly, the Caltrans attorneys argued that Surie's aneurysm damaged his vision to the extent that he didn't see the phantom car coming. The truth is, Surie had some vision loss after the aneurysm, but he had successfully passed the required driving class for people with brain injuries. The classes taught techniques to compensate for vision loss, which worked well for him. The judge responded the same as he had toward the first motion. Again, Caltrans' attorneys failed to produce a doctor to testify to this allegation. Their second motion was denied.

Thirdly, the Caltrans attorneys spent a lot of money and time producing a video that re-created the car crash. They had two different versions—one with a guardrail in place and a second without. Surprisingly, in both versions they did not include the burgundy car that started the chain of events. Consequently, the first version looked as though Surie had hit the guardrail for no apparent reason. In the second version of the re-creation, they attempted to show that even with a guardrail in place, my sons would have still passed. They showed our truck hitting a fabricated guardrail, the guardrail giving way, and our car falling in the very same location and position as it had fallen without a guardrail. The judge's response was classic. I don't remember his exact words, but he said something like this:

"I'm no rocket scientist, but do you mean to tell me that even if there was a guardrail in place, the impact would not have slowed down the Alexander's truck at all? Their truck still would have fallen in the same exact place if there was a guardrail? First of all, the Alexander's truck wasn't going fast enough to knock over a guardrail. Secondly, the truck would have slowed down to some degree from the impact of a guardrail. Maybe the truck would have slid down the hill instead of careening off the highway. The courtroom is where we separate facts from fiction. You can't show the jurors your false interpretation of the crash." He denied their video as evidence.

Now that the attorneys knew which motions would and would not be granted, they reevaluated their cases and prepared for the jury selection process. More than seventy potential jurors filled the courtroom. When the judge explained to the jurors that the trial was about the death of Murice and Roger, Surie broke down. The judge also told them the trial would be very interesting and should last about six weeks.

On Thursday, the jury selection process began. It felt strange as Surie and I walked past the jurors, who lined both sides of the hallway. I could feel them staring at us. We were not allowed to speak, gesture, or have any type of verbal or nonverbal communication with them. So for fear of jeopardizing our own case, we didn't even return a nod.

I prayed that God would touch every soul that entered that courtroom. I prayed for a supernatural miracle and for everyone involved to be blessed. I asked for God's favor and for His will to be done swiftly.

On Friday, our trial was not in session. Before the jury selection began on Monday, the third day of the trial, the Caltrans attorneys requested a meeting with the judge in his chambers. Our attorneys joined them. A half hour later, they emerged from behind closed doors. Our attorneys had good news. Caltrans wanted to settle! The jurors were thanked and dismissed for their time and service, and then the trial was dismissed.

"Praise God and thank you, Jesus!" I shouted quietly.

Over the weekend, the attorneys on both sides had reassessed their cases. The Caltrans attorneys realized that the three main weapons they had formed against us would not prosper. They had no choice but to bail out and bow down to the prayers of God. God's will was done swiftly and with fairness. It was over before it began. We settled our case, and that also took care of Angelina's case, which was contingent upon the result of our trial.

Some people thought I would have a hard time forgiving Surie. I didn't have to forgive my husband because I didn't blame him. Neither did the district attorney. All charges against Surie were dismissed. Wow, the power of prayer—it sure does change things!

> *No weapon formed against you shall prosper, and every tongue*
> *which rises against you in judgment you shall condemn.*
> *This is the heritage of the servants of the LORD, and their*
> *righteousness is from Me," says the LORD.*
> —Isaiah 54:17

CHAPTER FIFTEEN

ACHIEVING OUR DREAMS

"Help others achieve their dreams and you will achieve yours."

In 2001, we attempted to adopt Angelina, but once she was reunited with her sister, Felicity, the county social worker understandably did not want to separate them. They were now a package deal. If we adopted one, we would have to adopt the other. The problem was, Felicity had personal needs that required more structured living arrangements than we could offer. After three years as parents to Angelina and almost one year with Felicity, we had tried everything to make it work, but regrettably it wasn't meant to be and they moved on. So now, after eleven years, Angela was our only child again.

Being foster parents with Childhelp USA was such a rewarding experience for each member of my family. We started off giving and ended up on the receiving end of pure love and joy from adorable children. In addition to Angelina, Roger, and Felicity, we've cared for many other children throughout the years. During times when we were in need of healing, it helped us to care for others. However, in order to give ourselves adequate time to share our amazing testimony, we decided to forgo being long-term foster parents. The agency reassigned us to respite care, which provides emergency care and relief for foster families.

Two years later, in March 2003, our social worker called to inform us that there was a little girl who needed a home. We were surprised she contacted us since we were only available for temporary care.

"I'm sorry, but we're no longer long-term foster parents," I reminded her.

Our social worker knew our status, was aware of our testimony, understood our situation, and respected our decision to be categorized as a respite care foster family. So once she was reminded of those facts, she altered her question.

"Can she just come over for a couple of days? She needs to be moved right away, and that will give us time to find her long-term placement in another home. Her foster mother is having a complicated pregnancy and she's on doctor's orders not to lift over ten pounds."

Once again, I instantly began trying to see if I could make it work on a long-term basis.

"Well, how old is she? Can she go to school so I can still have my days available?"

"She's fourteen months."

"Fourteen months! No way—that's a baby in diapers!"

I was so busy I didn't have time to care for an infant. The phone went quiet. Neither one of us said anything for a while. Our social workers knew we had a soft spot in our hearts for children.

"I need to speak with my husband, and I'll call you back," I said, breaking the silence.

I walked into our bedroom and told Surie the foster agency had just called. From the look in my eyes, which he had seen on many occasions, he immediately knew.

"No, no, no, Angela. I like the calmness in our home, and I don't want to share you anymore," Surie told me upon hearing the situation.

"Surie, I know, and I truly feel you; however, this little girl is in an emergency situation and needs to move tomorrow. The social worker asked if she could come over for just a couple of days while they screen other homes."

At first, Surie didn't say a word. Then he hesitantly and very s-l-o-w-l-y whispered, "Yes, but only for a couple of days. And get that in writing!" he asserted.

I called the social worker back and let her know the little girl could come as long as it was only for two days and added, "Please pick her up no later than noon on Thursday because I have an important 2:00 p.m. appointment to attend."

Our social worker was very, very appreciative.

"I'll bring Angela over tomorrow. In the meantime, I'll diligently search for another home for her."

"Wait a minute. Wait a minute. What did you say?" I needed to hear that name again.

"Oh, didn't I tell you her name is Angela?"

"No, stop kidding! Her name is not Angela. I already said she could come over."

When I told Surie her name was Angela, we both just laughed.

"Angela, Angela, Angela. God, is there a shortage of names in this world? I now have three Angelas. This time I won't need speech, but mental, therapy," Surie said, laughing.

"God got jokes!" was all I could say.

The next day, we picked up Baby Angela from the foster agency. As we drove, we couldn't stop looking at her, and she at us. Before we arrived home, Baby Angela had captured our hearts, and once again we found ourselves tangled in another love triangle.

Alice's daughter, Lareina, was spending the school year with us. She and Angela were home from school when we arrived, and they too were instantly in love with this little girl. As cute as she was, her hair was a mess. Lareina—being the hair stylist that she is—immediately combed and braided Baby Angela's hair. Watching Lareina braid reminded me of her mother braiding my hair.

That same evening was Praise Outreach, where we share testimonies and sing praises to God. I shared that God had blessed us with a little girl. Of all the 365 days in the year, this one was very special—Angela was placed in our home on April 1, 2003, the third anniversary of Murice's and Roger's deaths. And out of all the names in the world, I told them, her name is Angela. That's another major miracle in action!

The next morning, the social worker came to take Baby Angela to a court appearance, where her biological mother would be present. When the social worker saw Baby Angela, she hardly recognized her with the new hairdo. She also observed the love between my family and the baby, especially the connection between her and Surie.

"My goodness, if I didn't know better, I would swear you were her biological parents," she declared.

Our hearts dropped when she informed us that Baby Angela had a new home and would be leaving the next day. Without any discussion beforehand, Surie and I instantly expressed our desire to keep her.

"Impossible. It's too late," she informed us.

Nonetheless, she encouraged us to contact the county social worker assigned to Baby Angela's case to inform her of our wishes. Surie immediately handed me the telephone.

The county social worker simply restated the news we did not want to hear: "No, I've interviewed another family. They have already prepared their home and are currently awaiting Angela's arrival." With Surie nudging me to not take no for an answer, I convinced her to at least give us a home study visit as well.

"Angela is adoptable, and the other family has seriously considered that step," she let me know.

The pressure was on, and the ball was in our court. "We are also interested in adopting Angela," I heard myself say before I knew it.

Armed with that favorable information, she promised to schedule a visit with us before she made her final decision. The next day was Thursday. I cancelled that very important appointment I had without a second thought. For the home visit, an adoption social worker unexpectedly accompanied the county social worker. They witnessed the warmth in our home and our love for Baby Angela. They saw how she joyfully played and held on to Surie. They knew in their hearts that this was not only her new home but, more importantly, her new family and agreed that she could stay.

While they were happy to deliver the good news, they were nervous as well. Months before, another family had wanted to adopt Baby Angela, but once they learned of her medical history, they declined. It turned out that doctors were afraid she might have been born with the HIV virus. At birth, Baby Angela was placed on antibiotics and tested for AIDS. Praise God the test came back negative.

As the social workers explained their concerns, they watched our expressions for signs of doubt and reservations. They were delighted to see there were none. I truly believe that this medical scare was a camouflage God placed over Baby Angela to save her for us.

"If her next HIV test were to come back positive, what would you do?" the social worker questioned.

"We would do the same as if this happened to our other daughter Angela: pray and get the best medical help that we could," I boldly responded.

So with that major detail addressed, we started the paperwork for Baby Angela's adoption. I believe that sometimes we are the answers to other people's prayers—and babies have prayers too.

"Angela, how can you meet someone one day and make such a major decision to adopt the very next day?" my friends wondered. Once they met Baby Angela and saw the joy in her eyes, all of their questions and doubts were answered and put to rest.

When Baby Angela turned three years old, she no longer allowed us to address her as Baby Angela and brought it to our attention when we did. Wow, that changed things and made distinguishing one of us from the other even more complicated. But it helped Surie. Even with his speech deficit, he couldn't say the wrong name when referring to any of us. God is so strategic.

now when he calls "Angela," sometimes all ___er and sometimes no one does. People have ___ggested a variety of nicknames, such as Angela 123 or ABC; Big, Middle, Little; Original, Hot 'n' Spicy, and Extra Crispy—the list goes on and on. Please pray for us. It's very confusing.

Baby Angela is our gift from God—proof that our Lord restores. She didn't have to come through me to come to me. Love is thicker than blood, and we love her just as much as if she was our biological child. In June 2004, our adoption was complete. Baby Angela's name is now Angela Alicia Alexander. Her middle name is for my sister Alice. Doctors have tested Angela for the HIV virus several times over the years. Each time, the results have returned negative, and the doctors have declared her clear of the virus. Every time I say our name, "Angela," it reminds me of God's promise.

I will never leave you nor forsake you.

—Hebrews 13:5

∽

Restoration did not end there for us. The following year, my oldest daughter Angela experienced a miracle all her own. One day while in the eighth grade, one of her teachers said to the class, "When my daughter becomes old enough, she's going to attend a high school called Vivian Webb." Her teacher's daughter was only five years old at the time. That teacher's innocent statement was enough to intrigue Angela. She hurried home after school and spent a considerable amount of time researching this prestigious high school online.

"Mom, I want to go to this school called Webb, and I would have to become a boarding student. Can I go? Please, can I go?" she begged.

When I found out how much the tuition was, I looked at my daughter like she had gone crazy. "You will be in college three years from now, and then you can have your dorm life experience," I said to her.

Without saying anything, Angela went back upstairs, called the school, and spoke with one of the faculty members on the administrative staff. The next thing I knew, we were receiving information and brochures in the mail. The next month, someone from The Webb School called me.

"Are you aware that your daughter registered your family to attend our open house?" she asked me.

"Angela, what are you doing? Why did you register us to attend their open house?" I asked when she came home from school. I could tell by her response that she had prepared for this conversation.

"Mother, people from all over the world are making flight arrangements, booking hotels, and renting cars to attend Webb's open house, and we only live twenty minutes away. I checked your Air Force schedule and you don't have to work that weekend, and the open house doesn't cost anything to attend. I also called the babysitter and she's available," she confidently informed me.

I couldn't be mad at her. She had done her homework and was just being the Yes-I-can person we had always encouraged her to be. Throughout her life, she has heard me tell her in many ways to follow her dreams:

"What you want wants you."

"Miracles are always in action."

"You have not because you ask not."

"Where your attention goes, the energy flows."

"Do what you can; God will do what you can't."

"You don't discover your destiny, you uncover it."

"Where you think the longest, you think the strongest."

"Hope for the best and prepare for the desires of your heart."

"Spend more time on your own vision than your boss's vision."

"Don't allow your life's pivotal points to become your pitiful points."

"If you can achieve all of your goals this year, then they're not big enough."

"You have to have a dream in order to have a dream come true. However, some dreamers dream, while others wake up and achieve."

Angela put all of these sayings to the test. She was dreaming that elephant dream. One by one, my daughter went down her list and eliminated all my reasons for saying no.

As we drove down the highway to attend the school's open

house, I tried to figure out how I was going to let my daughter down easy. The auditorium was filled wall-to-wall with people. After the introductions of some of the faculty and staff, all of the potential female students and their families moved to another location on campus, where there was, again, standing room only. Although Surie and I walked at a normal pace, Angela ran ahead to secure three front-row seats. I saw the gleam in her eyes as her wings spread to the extreme. She was soaking everything up, like a fish that had been released back into the water, as she listened to the information and students' presentations. During the question-and-answer period, Angela's hand went up several times. Now she was not only accelerating but also striving to live abundantly outside the box.

Once I heard the detailed list of application requirements, I was no longer concerned about bursting my daughter's bubble—reality would. To apply, applicants were asked to submit their report cards from the previous three school years, provide written recommendations from their school's counselor and math and English teachers, take an SSAT test, and turn in a written essay. I worried that Angela's grades following the crash might disqualify her. I also had to fill out a four-page application. Each of these requirements had a specific due date. Additionally, parents and students were scheduled for separate interviews with an administrative faculty member.

This school offered everything, and more, of what Angela

had been believing for. During the application process, Angela was a freshman at our local public high school, which had over 3,700 students in attendance. The average class size of the private school was fifteen students, and there were around 350 students in the entire school. As I walked around the campus, my thoughts took me back to when I was a boarding student. In order to assist Angela with her dream, I realized I had to set the money issues aside. I truly wanted her to experience a high-quality education. So after we prayed about Angela attending this school, we chose to move forward with the admissions process.

Over the next several months, as we completed each required task, we prayed over the school. We posted the school's posters on Angela's bedroom wall and scheduled our plans around her attending Vivian Webb. We simply spoke our dreams into existence.

"Name it and claim it. Pack your bags, because you're moving on campus," I told her many times.

During the parents' interview, Surie and I were told there were only eight to ten openings for female sophomores. Hundreds had applied. Decisions would be made and everyone would receive a letter of notification in the mail, one way or the other, by March 10, 2004.

I prayed over my daughter: "Angela, when God has your name on a blessing, no one can touch it. So, at this point, even if thousands are applying for only one opening, it's yours.

Every day visualize yourself receiving the acceptance letter and attending this school. When God gives you favor, He opens doors that no one can close. There's no need for a vote or an election; it's called God's theocracy."

Excited, nervous, and confident all at the same time, Angela could hardly sit still. March 10 finally arrived. Angela ran into the house from school to find the letter. "Miss Angela T. Alexander" read the envelope covered with colorful stars.

"Oh, I hope they didn't place stars on the outside and say, 'Please try again next year,'" she nervously said.

When she opened the envelope, confetti jumped out, falling all over the place! The letter read:

Dear Angela,

Congratulations! On behalf of the students and faculty, I am honored to offer you admission to the Class of 2007..."

"Thank you, Jesus!" she shouted as she dropped the letter, ran outside, and fell to the ground.

But then there was a second letter addressed to the parents of Angela T. Alexander. You see, just because you are accepted doesn't mean you are admitted. Our letter assured us that Angela had secured a guaranteed seat until July 1, 2004. By that time, we would need to know how we were going to pay for her tuition. I had already completed the school's financial aid package and was placed on their waiting list. With so many existing students requesting tuition supplements, there was no way to know how much would be available for new students. If we were not able to work out the financial situation, another student would fill Angela's position. Her admittance centered on our ability to pay the tuition.

I searched the Internet for scholarships and grants. The problem was, either the scholarship deadlines had passed or the amount of money we needed exceeded what was available for high school students. I went into deep prayer:

Dear God, I know You are a God of abundance and more than enough. The amount of this tuition represents a huge mountain for me, Lord. However, if it's meant for Angela to attend this school, You have the power to move that mountain. I surrender all, and I put it in Your hands. Amen.

Since prayer without works is dead, I continued searching for tuition money over the next several months. Finally, I informed the school regarding my unsuccessful results and thanked them for considering Angela for this wonderful opportunity. The very next week, a representative from Webb called and shared that the faculty, staff, and even some of the students wanted Angela to attend. His next words were a godsend. He informed me that the school was offering Angela a grant. He said they had never had a student who made the initial call and that they loved her spunkiness, respected her tenacity, and admired her well-rounded achievements and personality. He ended by saying she would be great for The Webb School, and vice-versa.

I was so excited, I could hardly speak. I thanked him repeatedly. I could barely hang up the telephone for jumping for joy and thanking God for always being so good to me and supplying what I called manna money.

After Angela's admission was complete, she and I spoke with the eighth-grade teacher who started her on this quest. We wanted to let her know how God had used her. She was extremely surprised and pleased for Angela's exciting new future and wonderful opportunities. She couldn't believe her one sentence had sparked such a reaction and caused a life to be changed forever.

Angela moved onto Webb's campus on August 28, 2004. She has since graduated from Vivian Webb and now attends Wellesley College in Massachusetts. God is so faithful. With this miracle, I believe He was simply preparing Angela for what He has preserved her for. God knew Angela was going to both boarding schools. By giving us Baby Angela, He did not leave our home childless, and He filled that gaping hole in Surie's heart.

And my God shall supply all your need
according to His riches in glory by Christ Jesus.
—Philippians 4:19

At the time of our children's deaths, I had fifteen years in the military. I asked God if He would give me the strength to stay in the Air Force for another five years, after which I would retire and dedicate my life to sharing His testimony. God granted me that strength. However, due to the Iraq War, in 2004, when I had only one more year to complete, my retirement became uncertain. Because of the need for additional military personnel, President Bush activated the Stop-Loss Program in many career fields, one being mine—air cargo specialist. That meant that even if the terms of your enlistment contract were honorably completed, you still could not discharge or retire until the Stop-Loss Program was lifted in your career field.

I became concerned because my retirement date was approaching fast, and I wanted to be obedient. I prayed to the Lord, my personal Commander in Chief, for resolution. God had guided my military career from day one. He had kept me in His hands of protection from basic training through the destruction of the World Trade Centers and the resulting aftermath. In 2001, many of the reserve and guard units throughout the world were activated. It was a miracle mine was not, though we were placed on military alert.

Just a few months before my date of retirement, the Stop-Loss Program was partially lifted. I praised God when I finally found out my career field was among the minority on the list. While the window of blessings was open, I hurried up and began

my out-processing paperwork. I retired from the
May 2005. During my retirement ceremony, Serge
sang a beautiful rendition of "Available to You." I ᴗ simply
clearing my table of the military and foster parenting to make
myself available for God to use as He chooses. Now I serve
Miracles in Action, my ministry, with humility and a great sense
of responsibility.

Through my travels in the Air Force, I was able to fulfill my
dreams. I visited all the exotic locations and countries Lovell
had described when I was younger. Daily, I continue to walk
in expectation of receiving God's miracles. My life has proven
over and over again that miracles are always in action—and I
just love watching God work.

ᴗ

We're still waiting on some restorations, one being Surie's
speech. One day my neighbor called and asked if I had heard
Surie's message on our answering machine? I hadn't, so I called
my home to hear the message.

"Thank you for calling the Alexander's family. Sorry we
missed your call, but if you leave your name and address at the
sound of the beep, we'll be glad to call you back promptly."

I laughed so hard I had to take a few deep breaths before I
could play it again. It was obvious he had desperately tried to get
it right. Then he saw me laughing.

"What's funny?"

"I just listened to your message on the answering machine."

"What's the matter? Did I stutter?"

"As a matter of fact, you did, amongst other things."

"No, I didn't. I got my brain fixed. Have you made your appointment yet?"

So the restoration of his speech is still in process. In the meantime, we're making the best of it.

∽

Three people who were, and still are, very close to me left incredible good-bye messages and then had supposed accidental deaths. When I received condolence cards that began with "Sorry for your tragedy . . . " or "Sorry for your loss . . . ," I had a hard time relating these words to my situation. While I could feel the love and comfort being expressed by those offering their condolences, I knew that AMR were not lost; I knew where they were. And I knew it wasn't a tragedy. AMR's good-bye messages were a confirmation of God's divine design and a comfort to them and to those who were left behind. The tragedy would have been if I had remained disobedient and neglected to share this testimony, my ministry.

Pam's husband, Ray, and my sister-in-law Clara have since passed. Many people would call their deaths a tragedy. But after watching the quality of their lives deteriorate in their last few months due to multiple medical complications, I know that the shedding of this physical body, which we call death, is not the worst thing that can happen to you. Many people automatically attach the word tragedy to my testimony. Since God prepared AMR, I don't see it that way. We miss Alice, Murice, and Roger beyond words, but we are excited for them, that they're in heaven. I'm often asked about closure. I will have closure when I see my loved ones again. For right now, I have peace here on earth.

Your particular grief may be a separation or a divorce, loss of a job, death of a loved one or a pet. Whatever it is, you need to turn your hurt into your harvest, your mess into your message, your pain into your power, your power into your passion, your situation into your sanctuary, and your miracles into your ministry!

God is truly the source of my strength. From the simple slogan "The seventh child is the wonder child," a mustard seed of belief was planted and grew into a strong, abiding faith. That same faith gave me the courage and passion to share my life's journey. Looking back, life has given Surie and me many wonders and tests, and God has turned them all into wonderful testimonies. This experience hasn't made me somebody; it has made me somebody else. Through it all, Surie and I are still together and happily married. As Murice said in his letter, "That is good to me."

This is the day the Lord has made;
we will rejoice and be glad in it.

—Psalm 118

Baby Angela at two years old with Surie on adoption day, June 2004.

Our eldest daughter, Angela, at Wellesley College, April 2008.

Angela Alexander is a retired member of the United States Air Force Reserve who has served in the Philippines, Korea, Japan, Germany, Alaska, Hawaii, and several bases throughout the United States. She volunteers with her church's prison ministry and was a foster parent for many years. An inspirational speaker, Angela shares her testimony with audiences nationwide. She lives with her husband and children in Southern California.

To interview Angela, book her for speaking events, or learn more about how you can work with the principles in her book to turn pain into power and grief into peace, visit www. miraclesinaction.com.